5.50

S0-CFB-318

THE
VICTORIOUS
LIFE

REVISED & EXPANDED

JOHN COBLENTZ

Christian Light Publications, Inc.
Harrisonburg, Virginia 22802

THE VICTORIOUS LIFE REVISION

Christian Light Publications, Inc., Harrisonburg, Virginia 22802

©1992 by Christian Light Publications, Inc.

All rights reserved. Published 1992

Revision 2007

Printed in the United States of America

Sixth Printing, 2010

Cover photos: © iStockphoto.com

Cover design: David W. Miller

ISBN: 978-0-87813-652-0

CONTENTS

INTRODUCTION

Have you struggled in defeat as a Christian?

Does some temptation constantly haunt you? Are you living in bondage to fear? pride? lust? self-pity? anger?

The psalmist cried, "Order my steps in thy word: and let not any iniquity have dominion over me" (Psalm 119:133).

Is that your prayer too? If it is, read on. In the following pages, you will find practical, step-by-step guidance from God's Word, guidance that will show you how to live in victory over sin.

The steps to victory are not always easy. But they are right. They are backed by the God of Heaven. They are backed by all the resources of Heaven. And they are worth every difficulty because they lead us to Heaven. "He that overcometh shall inherit all things; and I will be his God, and he shall be my son" (Revelation 21:7).

PART I

DEALING WITH SIN

My first introduction to Russ and Gwen came through a desperate call from Russ. He and Gwen had been married for nearly fifteen years, but their marriage was in trouble. Russ had heard that I helped people with troubled marriages, and he wanted to talk.

After coming to my house, he poured out his story. He and Gwen had had conflict much of their marriage, but recently things had gotten worse. She no longer trusted him. She accused him of all sorts of things from cheating on her to being physically dangerous. In fact, she had placed a restraining order on him. He was barred from his own house. Furthermore, Gwen declared she was done with the marriage. She was getting a divorce.

Russ acknowledged that he was "not perfect." Many of Gwen's accusations and dissatisfaction in their marriage grew out of his weekend habits. Instead of going with her to church, he would go to his cabin in the woods, have some beers (though he denied getting drunk), and enjoy the weekend relaxing. Russ acknowledged he had made some unwise threats to Gwen when she became "totally unreasonable," but he denied ever having hurt Gwen, and *never* would he lay a finger on the children. The idea that she would put a restraining order on him was totally groundless, he said. He was convinced she had done it only to hurt him.

I start with this story to make an important point: *We live in a world of sin.* People violate God's ways. Sometimes we do exactly what we know we ought not to do, and other times we refuse to do what we know we ought to do. Russ and Gwen knew better. Russ didn't have to be told he was being selfish to spend his weekends alone at the cabin. Gwen knew it was wrong to get a divorce. She attended church regularly. Russ refused to go because the pastor had offended him. The more I heard of their story, the more tangled the interpersonal sins became.

2

Everyone seemed to be intent on following his own agenda regardless of how it hurt others. Of course, it was always the other person's fault.

When I think of people like Russ and Gwen, I realize that this is one couple, one marriage. How many more marriages are, like theirs, in the process of falling apart because of selfishness and sin? How many angry words, hateful attitudes, selfish desires, lustful plans, and hurtful actions are happening in my town alone in any twenty-four-hour period? Multiply that by all the towns and cities in the country. Spread that over the entire world. What a world of sin!

And it surely isn't hard to sin in such a world.

We sin, of course, because we have been sinned against, don't we? We never would do what Russ and Gwen did, would we?

The frightening thing about sin is that it lies much closer home than we want to admit. We really do need to talk about sin.

SIN

THE BIBLE GIVES A NUMBER of definitions for sin, offers lists of sins in both the Old Testament and the New, and illustrates sin in countless stories. The Bible starts with a perfect garden and concludes with a perfect Heaven, but in between are the sad tales of human sin. From the time Adam and Eve sinned so long ago to the prophecies of earthly conditions when Jesus returns, we see violations, disobedience, wicked scheming, wrong desires, hurtful actions, bad attitudes, and all the consequences that go with sin. The picture isn't pretty.

What is sin?

The Bible gives us a number of answers to this question. "Sin is the transgression of the law" (1 John 3:4). God tells us what is right and what is wrong in His Word, and His Word is law. God doesn't do this arbitrarily. His Word is the expression of His character. God *is* right. In Himself, He is the moral standard of everything. Stealing is wrong, in other words, not simply because God decided it is better than not stealing, but because it is contrary to the character of God to steal. Lying, adultery, selfishness, greed, stinginess, treachery, ingratitude, disrespect—these things go against who God is. They violate His truth, faithfulness, love, generosity, mercy, and kindness.

Sin is not simply a matter of what we do, but a matter of what we are because righteousness is not simply a matter of what God does, but a matter of who He is. When we sin, then, we are violating God, and we are violating ourselves. We are walking across who He is, and we are desecrating who we are to be. He is righteous, loving, honorable, gracious, and true. And He created us in His image. Not exactly like Him, but a "finite image of the infinite God."[1] Sin transgresses what God has said, but it also desecrates what God has made us to be.

The Bible also says, "Therefore to him that knoweth to do good, and doeth it not, to him it is sin" (James 4:17). Sin is not just doing wrong, but failing to do what is right. Sometimes we refer to these two kinds of sin as sins of commission (doing wrong) and sins of omission (failing to do right).

It is sin to lie, but it is also sin to be silent when the right thing is to speak up (Proverbs 24:11, 12). It is a sin to steal, but it is also a sin to refuse to give what we have to someone who is in need at our doorstep (Luke 16:20; Proverbs 21:13). It is a sin to commit adultery, but it is also a sin not to love one's companion or to withhold marital kindness (1 Corinthians 7:5).

We must think of sin, therefore, not only in light of what we are forbidden to do, but also in light of what we are commanded to do. We are called to love God with all our heart, to love our neighbor as ourselves, to show kindness to our enemies, to pray for our leaders, to submit to one another, to pray without ceasing, to seek first the kingdom of God, to lay up treasure in Heaven, to care for the poor and downtrodden, to edify one another, and to do all to the glory of God!

"Therefore to him that knoweth to do good, and doeth it not, to him it is sin." How easily we measure sin by what we don't do wrong and forget about what we don't do right. The standard of righteousness is beyond any human being, and how true the evaluation of God is! "There is none that doeth good, no, not one"! (Romans 3:12).

Finally, the Bible says, "Whatsoever is not of faith is sin" (Romans 14:23). This simply means we are to live out of our trust in, and dependence on, God rather than in denial of, or indifference to, God. We are to make our decisions out of faith in God, not out of doubt or unbelief.

The person who has come to know God must not one day be guided by that faith and the next day be guided by doubts about God. He must not one day forsake dens of impurity because he knows God

6

disapproves of the lust and immorality in those places and the next day go into those places because he wonders if God even notices.

All Christians sometimes struggle with feeling the presence of God and wonder if God exists or cares for them. This verse is not demanding that we always confidently feel our faith, or that no thoughts of doubt ever pass through our minds. What this verse calls for is that we order our lives, make our decisions, and base our actions on our faith, not on those passing doubts. It means that our faith in God will keep us from stealing even though we may feel like stealing, keep us from committing adultery even though we may feel like committing adultery, and keep us from lying even though we may feel like lying. Likewise, our faith will urge us to be kind, to pray, to worship, to express gratitude, and to show respect even when we do not really feel like doing so because we know the former things are wrong and the latter things are right. Our faith guides us, and "whatsoever is not of faith is sin."

The Bible teaches us our sinfulness. And even if we did not have the Bible, we would have only to look about us to see how universal and pervasive sin is. Observe children on a playground, and it is not hard to spot selfishness, pride, unkindness, rivalry, and fighting. Observe adults in any organization, and unfortunately, we too quickly see the same sins. Look at nations, look at any history text, read the newspapers. Sin. Sin. Sin. It is written in large letters on what we have done, on our relationships, and on what we intend to do.

REPENTANCE

FORTUNATELY, THE BIBLE does more than describe our sin. It shows us what to do about sin. God offers pardon for sin. He has gone to incredible ends to arrange for our forgiveness. But there are conditions.

Sinners are consistently called by God to repentance. "Therefore I will judge you, O house of Israel, every one according to his ways, saith the Lord GOD. Repent, and turn yourselves from all your transgressions; so iniquity shall not be your ruin. Cast away from you all your transgressions, whereby ye have transgressed; and make you a new heart and a new spirit: for why will ye die, O house of Israel? For I have no pleasure in the death of him that dieth, saith the Lord GOD: wherefore turn yourselves, and live ye" (Ezekiel 18:30-32).

In the New Testament, Matthew records both John the Baptist and Jesus as proclaiming the call to repentance. "In those days came John the Baptist, preaching in the wilderness of Judaea, and saying, Repent ye: for the kingdom of heaven is at hand" (3:1, 2). "From that time Jesus began to preach, and to say, Repent: for the kingdom of heaven is at hand" (4:17).

As these verses indicate, repentance is a right response to sin, and repentance involves both attitude and action. The attitude of repentance includes submission as well as sorrow. It is the state of mind that recognizes we are wrong and God is right and a corresponding sorrow for what we have done.

The attitude of repentance breaks the heart with remorse, floods the eyes with tears, and casts the soul on the mercy of God. It is not an affected grief, but a thoroughgoing sorrow that comes from awareness of who God is, who we are, what we have done, and what we justly deserve.

The action of repentance involves a turning. We turn from disobedience to obedience, from resisting God to full submission, from choosing our own way

9

to wanting His way, from a bent toward sin to a hunger for righteousness. The sinner who was walking in the path of sin comes to a settled awareness that this path is wrong. Does he continue in the same path? God forbid! He turns around. He seeks the right path. He no longer wishes to go in the direction he was going, for he is assured it leads to misery and destruction. Like a man traveling west who discovers he has traveled for hours in the eastbound lane, he seeks the quickest exit to reverse his direction, and he wonders how he could have been so stupid to have wasted all that time going the wrong direction. Repentance from sin is no less a turning, for it is a more tragic situation. Sinful living squanders not hours, but years. It is not harmless, inconvenient travel in the wrong direction, but willful violation of the ways of God. We are not merely frustrated or embarrassed about the loss of time, but brokenhearted for our rebellion and pride.

The right response to sin is repentance. When the people listened to Peter's sermon at Pentecost, they were "pricked in their heart," and they cried out for direction. Peter was not slow to reply. "Repent, and be baptized every one of you in the name of Jesus Christ for the remission of sins, and ye shall receive the gift of the Holy Ghost" (Acts 2:38).

God hates sin, but God is moved by repentance. The tears of sorrow, the broken heart, the yearning for another way—these signs of repentance open the floodgates of heaven's mercy. "For thus saith the high and lofty One that inhabiteth eternity, whose name is Holy; I dwell in the high and holy place, with him also that is of a contrite and humble spirit, to revive the spirit of the humble, and to revive the heart of the contrite ones" (Isaiah 57:15). And in his psalm of penitence, David writes, "The sacrifices of God are a broken spirit: a broken and a contrite heart, O God, thou wilt not despise" (Psalm 51:17).

Sin is defacing to the image of God in man. It violates character, turns a person into an animal, ruins lives, and wrecks relationships.

David—a man after God's own heart—lusted after another man's wife, took her for his own gratification, and got her pregnant. This sin led to lies, treachery, and murder to cover up his immorality. The man who had led God's people to new heights politically and spiritually fell to this ugly level of selfishness and sin. He brought shame to the name of God, embarrassment to his family, disgust to his closest friends, and confusion to the nation. Sin is ugly.

But David repented. He saw his sin for what it was, and the sight broke his heart. Before God he poured out his sorrow, his yearning for cleansing, and his desire to return to the right path. "Create in me a clean heart, O God; and renew a right spirit within me. Restore unto me the joy of thy salvation; and uphold me with thy free spirit" (Psalm 51:10, 12).

God was moved by David's repentance, and God forgave David's sin.

Manasseh was the most wicked of the kings of Judah. His slide into idolatry included sexual rituals and child sacrifice. He built altars to these idols and set them up in the temple. He practiced witchcraft. Furthermore, he compelled the people of Jerusalem to follow his ways and he oppressed and killed those who wished to live right. So horrible and wicked was this king, that God declared the destruction of Jerusalem was inevitable. Against this wicked king the Lord brought the army of Assyria, who "took Manasseh with [nose] hooks, bound him with bronze fetters, and carried him off to Babylon" (2 Chronicles 33:11, NKJV).

The price of darkness is terrible! But the tragic consequences of his sin brought this wicked man to

12

his knees. The Biblical record goes on to say, "And when he was in affliction, he besought the LORD his God, and humbled himself greatly before the God of his fathers, and prayed unto him" (vv. 12, 13). How will a righteous God respond to such a wicked man? The incredible words of Scripture continue, "And when he prayed to him, the Lord was moved by his entreaty and listened to his plea" (v. 13, NIV).

God truly is moved by a broken, penitent heart. To all these stories of wickedness and redemption, we could each add our own. No matter how sinful we have been, we are lost without the mercy and grace of God. All have sinned. And all must repent to be saved.

CONFESSION

AN INTEGRAL PART OF REPENTANCE is confession. How often have people fallen short of full repentance because they have not been willing to name their sins honestly? We want to explore what confession is, look at some pointers for making proper confession, and then give some cautions and clarifications about confession.

What is confession?

"If we confess our sins, he is faithful and just to for-give us our sins, and to cleanse us from all unright-eousness" (1 John 1:9).

"Confess your faults one to another, and pray one for another" (James 5:16).

The Greek word translated *confess* is made up of two word parts. One means "to say," the other means "same." A strict rendering of the word parts would be "samesay." A more understandable translation would be "to say the same thing" or "to agree."

Confession, then, is a verbal agreement with truth. Though it is commonly used in relation to the truth about wrongdoing, it may be used in relation to any truth. Jesus Christ is Lord. That is truth. The confes-sion of that truth is part of becoming saved (Romans 10:9).

In the same way, to confess our sins is to say the truth about them. No more, no less, just the honest truth. If I am holding a grudge, I confess that by saying, "I am holding a grudge." To say, "I have had an attitude" is evading a direct confession. Too many people fail to find cleansing and deliverance from sin because they protect it under the cover of a general, unspecific confession. They want to salve their conscience, but they don't really intend to renounce the sin and be done with it.

"He that covereth his sins shall not prosper: but whoso confesseth and forsaketh them shall have mercy" (Proverbs 28:13).

How do I make a proper confession?

The Bible names a great many sins. There are sins of action, sins of speech, sins of thought and mind, and sins of heart and attitude. There are sins of commission and sins of omission, sins of the flesh and sins of the spirit, willful sins and sins done in ignorance. There are open sins we can easily point to and hidden imperfections in our character which we see only as through a fog.

How do we deal with these sins? Are we required to name everything wrong in our lives? The following pointers from the Scripture will help us see what God expects of us in confessing our sins.

1. Walk in close fellowship with God.

"God is light, and in him is no darkness at all. If we say that we have fellowship with him, and walk in

darkness, we lie, and do not the truth: but if we walk in the light, as he is in the light, we have fellowship one with another, and the blood of Jesus Christ his Son cleanseth us from all sin. If we say that we have no sin, we deceive ourselves, and the truth is not in us. If we confess our sins, he is faithful and just to forgive us our sins, and to cleanse us from all unrighteousness" (1 John 1:5-9).

Let's follow the train of thought that leads up to the instruction to confess: God is light. There is not the least shadow of iniquity in God. Man, however, is altogether different. All have sinned. Even after we are born again and no longer walk in sin, we do at times "miss the mark" (the literal meaning of *sin*). If we walk in the Light, these sins are revealed. To deny our sins in such a revealing Light is to lie.

So when you sin, confess it. Agree with truth. Don't deny anything revealed to you in the light of fellowship with God.

2. Name the sin clearly and specifically.

If in the light of God we see that a comment we made was unkind, that unkind comment needs to be named for what it is.

Our wrong words and actions, however, are often but the expression of a deeper problem in the heart.

Suppose, for example, Jack is not elected to a certain church committee. He comments irritably to Sam, "What good do elections do? You people just vote for your friends anyhow, instead of considering qualifications."

Later, Jack feels guilty and wants to make things right. What is his sin? If he confesses that he spoke unkindly, he has named a sin for sure, but if he names that sin only, he has dealt with a symptom, not the root problem.

If Jack walks in the Light, if he opens his heart honestly to God, he will see that underneath his unkind comment was a wrong attitude. Was it selfish ambition? Was it pride? If he wants to deal thoroughly with his sin, he needs to agree with "the truth, the whole truth, and nothing but the truth." Until he deals with the underlying attitude, it will continue to find expression—perhaps in more unkind comments, in uncooperative behavior, in gossip and grudges.

Here, then, is a simple rule for such confessions: Name the root, then the fruit.

In Jack's case, this would mean saying something

like this: "God has shown me that I have been self-centered in wanting a position in the church. I have thought more about my position than about the good of others. As a result, I spoke unkindly to you, Sam, and accused you wrongly. Will you forgive me?"

With such a confession, Jack is naming his sin at the heart level (root) and also at the level where it found expression (fruit). This results in a cleansing experience for Jack, and it also makes it easier for Sam to extend forgiveness because he has the assurance that Jack's repentance is sincere and thorough.

3. Confess the sin to the correct individual.

"Against thee, thee only, have I sinned, and done this evil in thy sight" (Psalm 51:4).

"Confess your faults one to another, and pray one for another, that ye may be healed" (James 5:16).

All sin is against God. In David's adultery with Bathsheba, he sinned against Bathsheba, against Uriah her husband, against his own family, and against the nation of Israel. But all of this paled as David stood before the Majesty on high and realized that by this deed, he had brought "great occasion to the enemies of the Lord to blaspheme" (2 Samuel

12:14). Psalm 51 is David's confession to Jehovah.

When we sin, therefore, we must first clear the record with God. He is the supreme Lawgiver, and He is the supreme Forgiver.

Many sins are against others also. A sin against one's partner needs to be confessed to that partner. A sin against one's family needs to be confessed to the family. Private sins are dealt with in private, public sins in public. If Jack, in the former illustration, makes his unkind comment to Sam, to Sam he needs to confess it. If he makes it loudly so that the whole group hears, it is proper for him to make his confession in the same audience.

James encourages even more: "Confess your faults one to another." The context here would seem to indicate that there is benefit in confessing to fellow Christians one's faults (literally, "sideslips" here, including offenses, failures, or sins).

After Jack has cleared his conscience with Sam, in other words, he may benefit by confessing to fellow Christians his problem of pride. He need not go into the details of his tiff with Sam (unless that has become common knowledge), but there is value in opening his fault—his sidestep into pride—to other believers.

Such confessions "one to another" urge others on

19

in the way of holiness, demonstrate the abandonment of self, encourage a tenderness one toward another, and enable fellow Christians to "pray one for another" specifically and effectively.

4. Seek a clear conscience.

"If we confess our sins, he is faithful and just to forgive us our sins, and to cleanse us from all unrighteousness" (1 John 1:9).

The goal of confessing sin is to clear the conscience. The benefit of being specific and thorough in naming our sins is receiving thorough forgiveness for those specific sins.

In clearing up interpersonal offenses, it is especially important to keep in focus the goal of clearing the conscience. Sometimes people confess their sins with a goal to bettering the relationship—making Dad more considerate, for example, or making Jane more agreeable. The confession is made and Dad still gets angry. Jane still argues. "It didn't do any good," we conclude.

This is an unfortunate misunderstanding of the purpose of confession. True, sometimes relationships do improve when people confess their sins, but that must not be one's goal or expectation. The goal of confession is to clear the conscience. If wrong has been done, that wrong must be named as wrong in a clear confession.

What freedom it brings when we know that no one can point a finger and say, "You did this against me, and you never made it right!"

The freedom of a clear conscience is not only the inner release from guilt, however, but the freedom to testify to the truth on any subject. Those who have a clear conscience can speak freely to others about love, about honesty, about purity, about forgiveness, about anything in the Bible.

Remember Jack? Suppose he does *not* clear his conscience with Sam. What testimony can Jack give on the subject of kindness in our speech (Ephesians 4:31, 32), or on the subject of preferring others in honor (Romans 12:10)? By making a thorough confession, however, Jack can not only speak freely on these subjects, but can give personal testimony to their truth.

5. Confess in genuine sorrow.

"The sacrifices of God are a broken spirit: a broken and a contrite heart, O God, thou wilt not despise" (Psalm 51:17).

21

"For godly sorrow worketh repentance to salvation"
(2 Corinthians 7:10).

We have seen that the proper method of confession
is clearly naming one's sin to the correct individuals.
The proper attitude of confession, now, is brokenness.

Probably the number one hindrance to proper
confession is pride. Pride keeps us from being specific. Pride causes us to give reasons why we did
wrong. Pride urges us to measure our wrong against
the other person's wrong. (The other person's wrong
is invariably worse, in our way of thinking.) Pride
tries to make us a victim of circumstances. Pride may
even nudge us to point out good things that resulted
from our wrongdoing. Those who are willing to agree
with the truth of their sin will be broken. Brokenness
gives us freedom from all the pitfalls of pride.
Brokenness gives us the freedom to deal with sin
without delving into the sins of others. Brokenness
gives us the freedom to be honest.

6. Confess with the resolve to forsake sin.

*"He that covereth his sins shall not prosper: but
whoso confesseth and forsaketh them shall have
mercy" (Proverbs 28:13).*

Mere confession of sin is not enough. Some people confess their sins with short-term objectives only—to find relief from guilt, to impress others with their holiness, to get relief from conflict, or to avoid certain consequences. Some people, in fact, become experts at naming their wrongs at just the right time to get out of trouble. But they have no real intention of forsaking sin.

True confession is an agreement with truth—not only the truth about sin, but the truth about righteousness as well. Those who agree with the truth about their sin will likewise agree with the truth about God's ways, and they will desire to walk in those ways.

Is it possible to be overbalanced in confessing one's sins?

Any truth misunderstood can be dangerous. Every truth needs the balance of other truth. So having stressed the importance of confession, let's look now at a few balancing pointers.

1. Openness needs the balance of discretion.

"A fool uttereth all his mind: but a wise man keepeth it in till afterwards" (Proverbs 29:11).

"A prudent man concealeth knowledge: but the heart of fools proclaimeth foolishness" (Proverbs 12:23).

Openness needs the balance of discretion. God wants us to be honest about sin. He encourages us to confess our faults one to another. But He certainly doesn't intend that we walk around with our hearts turned inside out. To speak too often and too extensively about one's personal needs can make us overbearing and may actually be a covert way of seeking attention from others. Prudence would tell us:

a. It is unnecessary to share the same problem with numerous people.

b. Christians should be especially cautious about confessing personal needs and problems one-to-one between members of the opposite sex.

c. In group settings, some sins can be named specifically (such as adultery) but should not be described in detail.

d. It is unkind and unnecessary to confess negative feelings against others if those people have no idea the feelings were there.

Concerning this last point: to say to someone, for example, "I've been carrying a bad attitude toward you," when that person had no knowledge of your attitude, only amplifies the problem. If the person is puzzled or hurt, you have to give explanations that only drag him through the muck of your own heart. Now, if the attitude has found expression, by all means acknowledge the wrong words or actions along with the wrong attitude. But if the person is unaware of your problem, it is better to take care of it between you and God.

The same principle applies to confessing wrong attitudes in a group. If a person feels guilty for not liking certain people in the church and publicly confesses, "I've had bad attitudes toward certain people, and I ask for forgiveness," no one knows who those "certain people" might be or what they may have done wrong. Again, it is far better to clear this before God and not drag others into uneasiness through a "bad attitude" confession.

2. We must distinguish between the condition of guilt and guilt feelings.

"For if our heart condemn us, God is greater than our heart, and knoweth all things. Beloved, if our heart condemn us not, then have we confidence toward God" (1 John 3:20, 21).

When we do wrong, we are guilty of that wrong. That is our condition, no matter how we feel. Confession is the acknowledgement of that condition of guilt—we are called to agree with truth no matter how we feel about what we have done.

Just as we may not feel guilty when we really are guilty, so we may feel guilty when we really are not. Under the weight of guilt feelings, some people feel compelled to confess the same sin over and over or to confess trivial or even imagined offenses. They have unfortunately confused the condition of guilt with guilt feelings.

3. We must distinguish between the voice of God's Holy Spirit and the voice of a misguided conscience.

"And I will pray the Father, and he shall give you another Comforter, that he may abide with you for ever; even the Spirit of truth; whom the world cannot receive, because it seeth him not, neither knoweth him: but ye know him; for he dwelleth with you, and shall be in you" (John 14:16, 17).

God's Spirit is holy. He stands foursquare against sin. But He deals with the believer according to truth in love. Whether His work is instruction, encouragement, correction, or conviction, He operates as an indwelling Comforter, not as a Tormentor. (The Greek word is *paraklete*, meaning "advocate" or "one who stands in behalf of another.")

Some people sincerely want to do right but constantly live under the torment of having done some little thing wrong. They feel compelled to confess they lied, for example, when they said the time was three o'clock, and really it was 3:02. They worry so about such "lying" that they are afraid to make any positive statement, lest it be inaccurate. Such sensitivity is from a misguided conscience, not from the Holy Spirit of God. Wouldn't we consider a parent to be cruel who walked around with a heavy stick over the head of his child, whacking him every time he made such a trivial mistake? Be assured the Holy Spirit is no such tormentor either. Wiser than the wisest parent, He instructs us when we need direction, comforts us when we are distressed, and chastens us when we are wrong, but always as the indwelling Spirit of truth.

JUSTIFICATION

WHEN SINNERS BELIEVE the Word of God against sin, when they believe that God sent His Son to die for sinners, and when they act on that faith by confessing their sins to God in penitence, the results are wonderful in the true sense of that word—full of *wonder!*

1. God forgives!

God is the Judge of all the earth, and according to His verdict, all the world stands guilty before Him. Using courtroom terminology, Paul writes, "Now we know that what things soever the law saith, it saith to them who are under the law: that every mouth may be stopped, and all the world may become guilty before God" (Romans 3:19). A few verses later, he bluntly says, "For all have sinned, and come short of the glory of God" (v. 23).

How can a righteous God forgive sinners? Can He simply wipe the slate clean? Can He act as though they had never sinned? Would a righteous God pretend in such manner? The Scriptures are clear that God is righteous, that the sentence of a righteous God against sinners is death, and that no man can change what God has said.

God forgives, not by looking the other way, not by pretending something that is not so, but by sending His Son to die for sinners. Jesus was sinless. He is God's Son. For Jesus to die for us makes the forgiveness of God a righteous act. The sentence of God's law upon us was satisfied in the death of God's Son for us.

To experience God's forgiveness calls for faith on the part of the sinner. We must know that we have sinned. We must acknowledge that our sin is against God. And we must believe that the death of God's Son on the cross was on our behalf and that it is sufficient to forgive our sins. Those who come to God by faith experience cleansing through the shed blood of Jesus. Our faith is demonstrated in our coming to God, in our repentance of our sin, in our willingness to name our sins specifically, and in our confession of Jesus as the Son of God.

"If we confess our sins, he is faithful and just to forgive us our sins, and to cleanse us from all unrighteousness" (1 John 1:9). "That if thou shalt confess with thy mouth the Lord Jesus, and shalt believe in thine heart that God hath raised him from the dead, thou shalt be saved. For with the heart man believeth unto righteousness; and with the mouth confession is

made unto salvation" (Romans 10:9, 10).

2. God justifies!

When we come to God through faith in Jesus, our sins are forgiven. This takes care of our past—we are cleansed. But God does more. He counts us righteous. The Scriptural term is that He justifies us. To understand this properly, we need to realize that in the Greek language, the same word translated "righteous" has a verb form. In the noun form, the word is sometimes translated "just" and sometimes "righteous." Since there is no verb form for righteous, the term "justify" is used, but it means, if we may mangle the English language, that we are "righteousified." That is, we are declared righteous.

For believers, this is instantaneous, it is complete, and it is wonderful! We are counted righteous before God. The Greek word indicates an objective reality—on the record books of God, we are reckoned righteous. We "add up" righteous.

How can this be?

Paul explains it in detail in Romans 4. He uses Abraham as the prototype of justification. "Abraham believed God, and it was counted unto him for righteousness" (v. 3). Just as Abraham's faith was counted (credited, reckoned, added up) as righteousness, so our faith in Christ adds up in the same way. Abraham was not counted righteous "by works" of the law. The law had not even been given. Abraham was not counted righteous by circumcision, for he was not yet circumcised (see v. 10). Abraham's faith was what added up to righteousness on God's books.

"Now it was not written for his sake alone, that it was imputed to him; but for us also, to whom it shall be imputed, if we believe on him that raised up Jesus our Lord from the dead" (vv. 23, 24). When we believe in Jesus, our faith is credited to us as righteousness—we are justified, declared righteous in the sight of God. Glory to God!

This is exactly what Jesus said to the Jews who asked, "What shall we do, that we might work the works of God? Jesus answered and said unto them, This is the work of God, that ye believe on him whom he hath sent" (John 6:28, 29). The Father declares us righteous, not by works of the law, but by our faith.

Thus, the requirement for our justification is faith. The means of our justification, however, is the blood of Jesus. "Much more then, being now justified by his blood, we shall be saved from wrath through him"

(Romans 5:9). The blood of Jesus represents His life given for us. He was absolutely righteous. This blood—this life of the sinless Son of God—is the means of our justification. Because of who Jesus is (the Son of God) and because He gave His life for us, the Father can righteously declare us righteous. As Paul explains, "Being justified freely by his grace through the redemption that is in Christ Jesus: whom God hath set forth to be a propitiation through faith in his blood, to declare his righteousness for the remission of sins that are past, through the forbearance of God; to declare, I say, at this time his righteousness: that he might be just, and the justifier of him which believeth in Jesus" (Romans 3:24-26).

As a propitiation for our sins, Jesus is more than adequate. In contrast, animal sacrifices, although required under the Old Covenant, were inadequate—"For it is not possible that the blood of bulls and of goats should take away sins" (Hebrews 10:4). But as the Son of God, Jesus is "much more" than adequate. Because of His death for us, the Father can righteously justify us. Paul insists there is no unrighteousness in God's act of justifying those who believe in Jesus. Our sins are gone, and we are declared righteous! Instantaneously, we are fully ready to meet the Lord, even though the process of making us righteous has only begun.

Now remember, when God declares us sinful, we have nothing to say except to agree. No man or woman in the world can reverse the just sentence of God against sin. Even so, when God declares us righteous, we can accept what He says with full assurance that it is so. Nothing in all the realms of men or spirits can say otherwise. As Paul says, "Who shall lay any thing to the charge of God's elect? It is God that justifieth" (Romans 8:33). In other words, when God declares us righteous, no one can bring a charge against us that will stick.

There can be no progress in a victorious life until sin is dealt with according to the provisions of God through Christ. Furthermore, there can be no victory unless we have the settled assurance that Jesus' work in our behalf is sufficient and sure. This is the requirement of faith. "But without faith it is impossible to please him: for he that cometh to God must believe that he is, and that he is a rewarder of them that diligently seek him" (Hebrews 11:6). Without faith we are lost. By faith we are saved—forgiven of all our sins and justified in God's sight.

RESTITUTION

WHEN OUR SINS HAVE BEEN FORGIVEN and we are brought into the family of God, we are called to walk a different road. We forsake the road of sin for the road of holiness. We leave the life of unbelief and enter the life of faith. We turn from willful disobedience to glad obedience.

This does not mean we are perfect. Christians can and do fail. But the direction of their life is different—whereas before they walked away from God, now they walk with God. The intention of their heart is different—whereas before they were intent on doing their own will, now they are intent on doing the will of God. This change is the natural and essential result of true repentance and a living faith.

If faith in Christ has no evidence in a change in life—if it produces no works, no evidence, no fruit—it is a dead faith and will not save us. James sums it up well: "Even so faith, if it hath not works, is dead, being alone" (James 2:17). The "work" of faith is simply the action of faith. If we believe a burner is hot, we don't place our bare hand on it. If we believe in the law of gravity, we don't walk off the edge of a roof. Even so, if we believe there is a right and wrong, if we believe there is a Heaven and Hell, and if we believe in God, we act accordingly. This is a "living" faith in contrast to a dead faith.

Those who leave a life of sin often need to make things right from their past life. They may have stolen things from local stores. They may have cheated their boss. They may have been unfaithful to commitments they made. They may have injured other people. Some wrongs cannot be made right. If you destroyed a family heirloom, you may not be able to replace it. If you destroyed a person's reputation, you may not be able to repair it. If you took someone's virginity, you cannot give it back. But some of the first works of faith in a new believer are works of restitution.

What we have stolen, we return to the best of our ability. What we have damaged, we repair. Where we have wronged, we try to make right. This is called restitution.

In the Bible, we have a wonderful example in Zacchaeus. This man was a tax collector, and tax collectors were notorious for taking more than was required by law and pocketing the difference. In Jesus' day there was hardly a distinction between a "publican" and a "sinner."

When Zacchaeus received Jesus, right on the spot he said, "Behold, Lord, the half of my goods I give to the poor; and if I have taken any thing from any man by false accusation, I restore him fourfold" (Luke 19:8). This penitent man was ready to make restitution where he could. Jesus said Zacchaeus's restitution was clear evidence of his salvation. "This day is salvation come to this house" (v. 9).

The work of restitution did not save Zacchaeus, nor will it save us. Rather, it is the result of salvation. It demonstrates that a change of heart has truly taken place. When a man who has been in the habit of taking everything he can begins to give whenever he has opportunity, he has clearly had a change of heart. When a person who has slandered the reputation of others asks for forgiveness, does what he can to make amends, begins to speak kindly of others, and protects the reputation of others, his new responses declare that he is a new person. Again, the work of restitution doesn't save; it only points to the reality of salvation. Smoke doesn't create fire; it only tells us where the fire is. Or to use another analogy, Jesus said, "Ye shall know them by their fruits. Do men gather grapes of thorns, or figs of thistles? Even so every good tree bringeth forth good fruit; but a corrupt tree bringeth forth evil fruit. A good tree cannot bring forth evil fruit, neither can a corrupt tree bring forth good fruit" (Matthew 7:16-18). The action of faith is evidence of a change in the heart—the heart that has been truly broken by sin before God will do all it can to make past wrongs right.

Furthermore, the work of restitution does not burden the heart; it sets the heart free. Zacchaeus, in other words, did not give his money with downcast eyes, sorrowful for all it was costing him. Rather, the restitution of stolen goods rolled a huge burden off his back. He no longer needed to shift his eyes when he walked down the street. He had no urging to cross to the other side of the street to avoid a person he had taken advantage of. His conscience was clear, and his feet were light. He could look at anyone, talk to anyone, share his new faith with anyone. What freedom restitution brings to the heart!

Restitution also sets up a barrier against returning to sin. We don't know how many people Zacchaeus may have visited in the days that followed his encounter with Jesus. And we don't know who may have heard about Zacchaeus's change of heart. But we can be quite assured that many heard—the story was public enough that it circulated for many years and found its way into Luke's Gospel. As Zacchaeus did business in the weeks and years that followed, he may have been tempted at times to take advantage of others—after all, it had been a way of life. But Zacchaeus's restitution created a different set of expectations in his acquaintances. This man, who once took whatever he could for himself, now is generous and concerned about giving the other person a good deal. That new reputation, started by the work of restitution, called Zacchaeus to faithfully live up to his new reputation.

How do we know what to make right? One guide is to ask ourselves if there is anyone who could point to us and say, "You wronged me, and you never made it right." If a finger can justly be pointed at us, we ought to do what we can to set the matter straight. Here are some questions we might ask:

1. Did I take money or possessions that belonged to others?
2. Did I cheat others out of what was rightfully theirs?
3. Have I twisted information that leaves others under wrong impressions?
4. Have I slandered the reputation of others?
5. Did I turn in time (or bills) that did not

accurately represent what people owed me?

6. Have I purposely avoided taxes by failing to report income?

7. Have I injured people or left them in need without making it right to the best of my ability?

As in the realm of confession so in restitution, sometimes people struggle with being overly sensitive. They may struggle with whether they ought to talk to a former schoolteacher about misrepresenting something. Again, one guide is to evaluate if the action stands against you in the mind of the other person. We might also ask if the situation were reversed, would we want the other person to come to us to make the matter right? If there still are questions, particularly if we know we struggle with being oversensitive, we might do well to discuss our questions with a mature Christian friend or pastor.

The goal of restitution is to set the heart free, not to burden the heart. And a heart set free is a great blessing! As the psalmist said, "Blessed is he whose transgression is forgiven, whose sin is covered. Blessed is the man unto whom the LORD imputeth not iniquity, and in whose spirit there is no guile" (Psalm 32:1, 2).

PART II

EXPERIENCING CHRIST AS OUR LIFE

Lena grew up in a Christian community. When she was the proper age, she asked to be baptized so she could join the church along with her peers. And Lena had an intense desire to do right. In fact, her desire to do right drove her to do things, say things, and wear things to look just right. But for many years she had a nagging unrest in her heart.

The unrest finally drove her to seek help from a devout Christian lady. After hours of soul-searching, she finally realized she had been driven for years by self-righteousness. Her efforts were her own attempts to gain right standing with God. She had never really rested her soul on the work of Jesus, nor had He been the longing and love of her heart.

When Lena finally saw the light, she saw her miserable self-righteousness for what it was. She repented in brokenness and tears. And she found her Saviour.

How easily religious people slip into the trap of trying to live the Christian life in their own strength! This can happen even after we have begun in Christ. Like the Ephesians, we can leave our "first love" even while we continue to be zealous about doing right. After all, we want to be productive. We want to please our Lord. We want to be strong, holy people. But without realizing it, we can begin to neglect fellowship with Jesus. Then we begin to substitute fleshly efforts for true spiritual vitality. We have learned how to talk and act, and soon we are "doing the motions" regularly but neglecting true spirituality. We may hide our lack of heartfelt love behind religious masks. We give the appearance that things are going well, but like Lena, we are caught in the trap of self-righteousness.

This section leads us to the source of the Christian life. The journey is sometimes surprising, sometimes painful, but always rewarding!

THE CROSS—DEATH TO SELF

"IF ANY MAN WILL COME AFTER ME, let him deny himself, and take up his cross daily, and follow me. For whosoever will save his life shall lose it: but whosoever will lose his life for my sake, the same shall save it" (Luke 9:23, 24).

Christ calls every person who would follow Him to deny self. This call strikes at the heart of man's waywardness. "All we like sheep have gone astray; we have turned every one to his own way" (Isaiah 53:6). It is impossible to follow this new Master without renouncing the old. Self, like a rebel king, has usurped the throne of the heart. Nobody, *nobody,* can follow Christ without renouncing himself.

What does it mean to deny self?

To deny means to utterly renounce or disown. Christ is not calling for self-denial in the ascetic sense (the abstaining from this or that), but in the absolute sense—the denial of *self.* The ax must be laid to the root. We must deal with the culprit in charge. No man can serve two masters. Jesus does not call us to deny self because the Christian life goes better when

43

we do so, but because it is *impossible* to be a Christian apart from denying self. If Christ is to be our Lord, self-renunciation is a must. The only way we can be honest in seeking what Christ wants us to do is to give up living for what we want to do.

Jesus described this elsewhere as a death experience. "Except a corn of wheat fall into the ground and die, it abideth alone: but if it die, it bringeth forth much fruit" (John 12:24).

Paul, too, spoke of death as a prerequisite to experiencing Christ as our life. "I am crucified with Christ: nevertheless I live; yet not I, but Christ liveth in me: and the life which I now live in the flesh I live by the faith of the Son of God, who loved me, and gave himself for me" (Galatians 2:20).

In spite of these clear teachings, many people want the Christian life without meeting this basic requirement for receiving it—giving up the self-life! They want Christ *and* self. They want Christ without the cross.

What is the cross in practical experience?

"Knowing this, that our old man is crucified with him, that the body of sin might be destroyed, that

44

henceforth we should not serve sin. Likewise reckon ye also yourselves to be dead indeed unto sin, but alive unto God through Jesus Christ our Lord" (Romans 6:6, 11).

The cross was a place of pain and humiliation, but primarily, it was a means of death. The person who died on a cross said good-bye to friends and relatives, took nothing with him on the cross, left his former life completely behind. He died.

We can make the analogy for anyone who wants to follow Christ. He leaves his old life behind. Following Christ takes precedence over everything else now. He dies to his possessions, his friends, his reputation, and his own life. The former identity is reckoned dead—counted as in fact to be dead. Living for self is viewed as the old life; living for Christ is the new life.

The world has no attraction to a dead person. The pleasures of the world, the lusts of the world, the pride of the world, the things of the world mean nothing to a dead person.

Every person has his unique struggle with the cross. We typically have some activity, something we especially value, or some besetting habit or attitude

45

that needs to die. For one person it may be devotion to his work, for another it might be sports or recreation, and for another it could be a habit of anger or an attitude of superiority.

The human heart is capable of setting itself on virtually anything and turning it into the thing his life revolves around. Death to self is invariably tied to these practical expressions of the self-life.

The Apostle Paul lived for "righteousness through the law." In Philippians 3, he describes his former life (his "old man") in terms of his Jewish pedigree, his zeal in performing all that the law required, his membership in the strictest Jewish sect, and his opposition to anyone who stood in his way (see vv. 4-6). When Paul met Jesus in that blinding encounter on the Road to Damascus, he needed to die to that former way of life. It was a difficult experience. The Jewish traditions were embedded deeply into his habits, his values, his attitudes, his life goals, and his daily activities. And what made Paul's past even more difficult to give up was that it seemed so good. It didn't seem to be sinful. Rather it seemed the opposite—Paul had a strong devotion to "righteousness." But it was rooted in himself, and it had to go.

Paul says when he met Jesus, he counted all this

former life "but loss," and even worse than that, he counted it "but dung." That's strong language. But the cross is a radical experience. When we consider how devoted Paul was to the Jewish traditions, we realize why this experience is referred to as a death. But Paul's experience is no different from the death we are called to today.

The person who has "lived for" his business— breathed it, ate and drank it, sacrificed for it, laughed and cried over its gain and loss—must die to business. The person who has lived for recreation or fashion or lands or the night life or women or music or wine must die to his old life in order to receive the life of Jesus. Likewise, the person who lives for religious tradition must die to it, for as with Paul, that can be nothing more than the "pride of life," the outworking of the self-life. Whatever we have set our hearts upon other than Christ or more than Christ must go to the cross.

Why is this death to self so important?

"Therefore we are buried with him by baptism into death: that like as Christ was raised up from the dead by the glory of the Father, even so we also should

47

walk in newness of life. For if we have been planted together in the likeness of his death, we shall be also in the likeness of his resurrection" (Romans 6:4, 5).

Death to self is the only gateway to life in Christ. This is a divine law as unchanging as the natural law of gravity. To live unto God, we must die to ourselves.

The reason this death to self is so important to us, however, is because this is our part. God calls us to surrender to the death experience—for that we are held responsible. He will take care of giving us life, but we must be willing to die.

It was so with Christ. He was responsible to go to the cross. He struggled in the garden with the awfulness of that death. But He surrendered, and He died. The Father answered with the resurrection.

Everyone who would follow in Christ's steps will experience the same sequence. Death must precede life. Our struggle is with the death experience—the renunciation of self, the dying to the old life and its ways. But everyone who says yes to the cross will be answered from Heaven with a new life. God's life always flows into those who die with Christ. It is a divine law.

What does it mean to experience Christ as our life?

"Abide in me, and I in you. As the branch cannot bear fruit of itself, except it abide in the vine; no more can ye, except ye abide in me. I am the vine, ye are the branches: He that abideth in me, and I in him, the same bringeth forth much fruit: for without me ye can do nothing" (John 15:4, 5).

The Christian life is not, as many think, just a matter of doing certain right things and avoiding certain wrong things. The Christian life is union with Christ. It is the experience of Christ living His life in us. We are united to Him in such a way that all our life comes from Him—like a branch joined to a vine. All the branch's vitality, nutrients, productivity—its very life—comes through the vine. The hope of growing and producing fruit is not a matter of the branch trying harder, but of simply opening up more to the life and nourishment of the vine.

So it is for the believer in Christ. Spiritual growth, spiritual vitality, spiritual productivity depend on union with Christ. He is our *life*. Without Him we can do *nothing*.

How many times Christians strain at improving

themselves, plan more religious activities into their schedule, resolve to overcome some bad habit, all without realizing that apart from Christ, all such efforts change nothing!

Don't misunderstand. Union with Christ includes labor, planning, and resolve. But it is labor by His strength, planning under His guidance, and resolve according to His purpose. The conscious awareness of Christ's presence and *dependence on Him* becomes the very life of the believer.

Jesus living in the believer, then, does not obliterate the believer. He does not make us inactive or reduce us to nothing. Rather, He engages us. He lives in and through all we are and do. He does not replace who we are, but by Him in us, we become who we were intended to be. He enters into our speech, our actions, our thoughts, our attitudes, our plans, our friendships, and our habits. His living presence in us deepens our thoughts, sweetens our words, guides our actions, and enriches our interactions with other people.

Life before Christ in us was the "old man," the old person who lived and thought for himself and in that Christless existence did many things against God and other people. Life in Christ, or life infused with

Christ, is the "new man," the new person who "walks" with Jesus and experiences Jesus in everything he does.

In Christ we become alive to a whole new realm of reality. The Scriptures refer to this as "alive unto God through Jesus Christ our Lord." (Romans 6:11). We see things we never saw before—the change is so radical that we refer to our former condition as "blind." Paul describes us as "having the understanding darkened, being alienated from the life of God through the ignorance that is in them, because of the blindness of their heart" (Ephesians 4:18). In Christ, our eyes are opened to God. We see His character, His purposes, and His ways. We are aware of His presence in our lives, and we observe that He works in our behalf. Whereas before, we ate His food, breathed His air, benefited in countless ways every day from His goodness—but were totally uncomprehending of Him—now we receive nothing without realizing it is from His hand. He is our Provider, our Protector, our Companion, and our Friend.

Life in Jesus is life in God. The Apostle John sums it up well: "And we know that the Son of God is come, and hath given us an understanding, that we may know him that is true, and we are in him that is true, even in his Son Jesus Christ. This is the true God, and eternal life" (1 John 5:20).

THE CLOSET—
DEVOTION TO GOD

"BUT THOU, WHEN THOU PRAYEST, enter into thy closet, and when thou hast shut thy door, pray to thy Father which is in secret; and thy Father which seeth in secret shall reward thee openly" (Matthew 6:6).

"Behold, I stand at the door, and knock: if any man hear my voice, and open the door, I will come in to him, and will sup with him, and he with me" (Revelation 3:20).

"The hour cometh, and now is, when the true worshippers shall worship the Father in spirit and in truth: for the Father seeketh such to worship him. God is [no a in Greek] Spirit: and they that worship him must worship him in spirit and in truth" (John 4:23, 24).

Every believer needs to spend time with God regularly. Worship, prayer, and Bible study are means of spirit-to-Spirit fellowship with God. This inner communion with the Lord builds our relationship with Him, provides us with spiritual nourishment, purges us of that which is carnal and worldly, and deepens our spiritual insight.

Many believers acknowledge the importance of spending time with God, but they struggle with actually doing it.

How can one's devotional time be meaningful?

"The eyes of the LORD run to and fro throughout the whole earth, to shew himself strong in the behalf of them whose heart is perfect toward [fully devoted to] him" (2 Chronicles 16:9).

"Devotional time," that is, time spent in prayer and Bible study, is easily misunderstood. Every Christian must learn this: God's primary concern is not with our devotional time, but with our devotion. Devotion is the bedrock of devotions. God draws near to those who are devoted to Him, but those who are not fully devoted may read the Bible and pray till they are blue in the face, and it impresses God not in the least.

We will consider some practical pointers in a moment, but make no mistake. No technique, no

Bible reading program, no devotional guide will ever substitute for a heart fully devoted to God. Some people (some very religious people) must understand, in other words, that they can never have a meaningful devotional time until they repent of the clutter of worldliness in their hearts, until they return to complete devotion to God.

"If I regard iniquity in my heart, the Lord will not hear me" (Psalm 66:18).

What are some hindrances to meaningful time with God?

"Love not the world, neither the things that are in the world. If any man love the world, the love of the Father is not in him. For all that is in the world, the lust of the flesh, and the lust of the eyes, and the pride of life, is not of the Father, but is of the world" (1 John 2:15, 16).

There is much in the world that is beautiful and appealing, much even that is necessary—food and clothing, work and education, government and institutions. But the world system pulls relentlessly on the heart of man, attracting the interest, filling up the schedule, calling for time and money and affection.

In the Western world probably the greatest hindrance to meaningful time with God is the fast pace of life. We are people of motion, people of activity, people of hurry, people of schedule, people occupied constantly with sights and sounds and gadgets and projects.

It takes quietness to learn to know God. "Be still, and know that I am God" (Psalm 46:10).

It takes time.

SLOW ME DOWN, LORD

Slow me down, Lord.

Ease the pounding of my heart by the quieting of my mind.

Steady my hurried pace with a vision of the eternal reach of time.

Give me, amid the confusion of the day, the calmness of the everlasting hills.

Break the tensions of my nerves and muscles with the soothing music of the singing streams that live in my memory.

Teach me the art of taking minute
vacations—of slowing down to look at a
flower, to chat with a friend, to pat a dog,
to smile at a child, to read a few lines
from a good book.

Slow me down, Lord, and inspire me to
send my roots deep into the soil of life's enduring
values, that I may grow toward my greater destiny.

Remind me each day that the race is not
always to the swift; that there is more to life
than increasing its speed.

Let me look upward to the towering oak
and know that it grew great and strong
because it grew slowly and well.

Wilferd A. Peterson

Busyness, however, is not the only effect of the
world's system. The things of the world tug at our
hearts. The "taste" of worldly things is not the same
as the "taste" of spiritual things. There is sparkle and
glitter and exhilaration in the world. There is fun and
laughter and diversion. Certainly not all fun is
wrong. But the heart occupied continually with

jumpy activities, thumpy music, and light-hearted banter may be hard put to spend an hour with God. It may even struggle spending ten minutes. Bible reading seems dull compared to the constant stimulation of the screen or the thrill of rides or the cacophony of noise we are bombarded with in the world's places of amusement.

To have meaningful time with God, we cannot be addicted to the world's pleasures. Again, this does not mean Christians do not smile or have fun. But it means we cannot live to please fleshly desires and expect to be thrilled in the closet. Christians who find themselves bored and drowsy in their closets, who can't find the deep pleasure of the presence of God, must take a hard look at whether they are drinking at the wrong fountains.

For some people, this will call for radical action. It may mean getting rid of a favorite form of media. Cold turkey. It may mean selling equipment. It may mean making particular places of amusement off-limits. Many in the Western church have fooled themselves into believing they can follow the desires of the flesh, love the things of the world, and still be wonderful Christians. Peter tells us, "Dearly beloved, I beseech you as strangers and pilgrims, abstain from fleshly lusts, which war against the soul" (1 Peter 2:11). Times change, but truth does not. We cannot expect to have a strong, vibrant devotion to God, or meaningful times with Him in the depths of our being, if we are dulling our hearts with worldly pleasures.

Those who really wish to know God will not fit well into the pace and lifestyle of Western culture. Modern schedules and priorities are geared to the love of the world, not to acquaintance with God.

What are some pointers for those who are willing to draw near to God?

"*Draw nigh to God, and he will draw nigh to you*" (*James 4:8*).

"*Evening, and morning, and at noon, will I pray, and cry aloud: and he shall hear my voice*" (*Psalm 55:17*).

"*O God, thou art my God; early will I seek thee: my soul thirsteth for thee, my flesh longeth for thee in a dry and thirsty land, where no water is*" (*Psalm 63:1*).

We have already noted the importance of a

devoted heart, without which devotional time is pointless. Here are a few pointers for the devoted:

1. *Set a regular time.* If we try to fit time with the Lord into our schedule at random, we usually will find such time crowded out instead.

2. *Balance schedule with flexibility.* It is good to set goals for reading, study, or memorization of the Scriptures. But it is good to vary the pace and activity from time to time. A goal of reading through Genesis in two weeks, for example, may be interrupted if you experience loss or grief and need to find other Scriptures for comfort.

3. *Use a notebook.* Record your insights, your spiritual goals, your struggles, God's solutions, and your prayers. Writing down these things can be helpful in understanding and retaining them. It can also be beneficial later, for our problems sometimes recur.

4. *Share your faith.* Spiritual exercise stimulates spiritual appetite. The more we share the life of God with others, in other words, the richer it becomes. And the richer our life in the closet, the richer will be our conversation on the street.

Spending time with God regularly opens the

channels for Christ to live His life in us. His thoughts become our thoughts. His plans become our plans. His values become our values. We live unto Him; He lives in us. Such a life is altogether different from the self-life. "Therefore if any man be in Christ, he is a new creature: old things are passed away; behold, all things are become new" (2 Corinthians 5:17).

What are specific projects to pursue in personal time with God?

There are a variety of Bible study projects that can be spiritually enriching. Following a course of study can give us something to look forward to, and depending on what we are experiencing, a project can be tailored to our spiritual need at the time. Here are some suggestions:

1. Study a character trait of God. Learning to know God is at the heart of all Bible study (or ought to be) and is the primary fountain of inspiration. Choose a particular attribute of God, and using a concordance, look up Scriptural references to that attribute. Copy the verses, study the context in which they occur, and record your findings. In Psalm 36, for example, we have a list of such attributes.

"Thy mercy, O LORD, is in the heavens; and thy faithfulness reacheth unto the clouds. Thy righteousness is like the great mountains; thy judgments are a great deep: O LORD, thou preservest man and beast. How excellent is thy lovingkindness, O God! therefore the children of men put their trust under the shadow of thy wings" (vv. 5-7). Here we have reference to God's mercy, faithfulness, righteousness, justice, and love. We can make a study of each of those attributes. What is God's mercy, for example? How does He show it? How does God's mercy affect me?

2. Categorize the proverbs. The Book of Proverbs is a collection of wise sayings from Solomon and other writers. Some sections of these proverbs especially move from one subject to another— our speech, our heart, our business dealings, family relationships, child training, the fear of the Lord, work ethics, friendship, etc. Going through the proverbs chapter by chapter and placing the proverbs in categories is a huge exposure to wisdom. And it provides a resource for us afterwards—when we want to find guidance on friendship, for example, we can go to

61

our compilation of proverbs and have a whole list of verses that address friendship.

3. Do a character study. You might pick a character you admire in the Bible, someone you wish to learn more about, or a person who demonstrated a problem similar to one you struggle with. Read the portions of the Bible that describe the person's life, and record your observations. Here are some questions that can guide you in a character study: 1) What were the conditions under which this person lived? 2) What responsibilities did this person have, and how did he/she fulfill them? 3) What was this person's relationship with God? 4) What tests did this person face, and how did he respond under testing? 5) How was this person changed through these experiences? 6) In what ways is this person a good example for me? 7) In what ways would I not want to follow this person's example?

4. Do a book study. Choose a book you would like to study. If you have not done a book study before, you might wish to choose a relatively short book—three to five chapters, for example. Use a Bible dictionary or Bible encyclopedia to

research issues like author, date, and reason for writing. But avoid the temptation to let scholars do all your work for you. After you have studied the background information, scan the book. Try to write in one sentence the author's main point. The second time through, read the book more carefully, looking for any statement by the writer about his purpose for writing. Then study the book chapter by chapter, dividing each chapter into its natural sections. As you study each section, ask careful questions, such as: What did this say to the original audience? What is the theme of this section? What are the commands? What are the promises? What are the timeless principles? If there are figures of speech, what do they mean? Finally, be sure to ask, what are the lessons for me in this passage of Scripture? As you ask these questions, record your observations. You will find that any portion of the Bible you spend time with in this way becomes a significant source of guidance and direction for you. As the psalmist said, "Thy word is a lamp unto my feet, and a light unto my path" (Psalm 119:105).

THE CHURCH—
FELLOWSHIP OF SAINTS

"IN WHOM ALL THE BUILDING fitly framed together groweth unto an holy temple in the Lord: in whom ye also are builded together for an habitation of God through the Spirit" (Ephesians 2:21, 22).

"Unto him be glory in the church by Christ Jesus throughout all ages, world without end. Amen" (Ephesians 3:21).

"And he gave some, apostles; and some, prophets; and some, evangelists; and some, pastors and teachers; for the perfecting of the saints, for the work of the ministry, for the edifying of the body of Christ: till we all come in the unity of the faith, and of the knowledge of the Son of God, unto a perfect man, unto the measure of the stature of the fulness of Christ: that we henceforth be no more children, tossed to and fro, and carried about with every wind of doctrine, by the sleight of men, and cunning craftiness, whereby they lie in wait to deceive" (Ephesians 4:11-14).

As we can see from these verses, the church exists for a number of reasons. First, it exists for the glory of God. It is the earthly place God has chosen to live. Where God's people assemble in Jesus' name, God makes Himself known. Even, according to the words of Jesus, "Where two or three are gathered together in my name, there am I in the midst of them" (Matthew 18:20).

As God meets with the assembled saints, there will be worship. His presence is great, high, weighty, and overwhelming to gathered believers; and they rightly break out in song, testimony, prayer, and adoring worship. The church, therefore, is a place of worship.

Another reason for the church is for the growth and spiritual development of believers. A spiritual nurturing takes place when God's people meet with one another. Not only is the presence of God worshiped in the assembly, but His Word is given in the collective setting. He gifts particular ones for preaching, teaching, and exhorting the believers. These "pastors and teachers" provide guidance, comfort, wisdom, correction, warning, and instruction for the day-to-day situations believers face.

The "building up," however, happens not only in the individual lives of the members. The whole assembly "grows up" in faith and maturity through the spiritual ministry of the members to one another.

It takes more than an individual believer to demonstrate the "stature of the fulness of Christ." It takes the "body of Christ," the members working together in fellowship, worship, and ministry to experience spiritual maturity and to demonstrate the life and character of Jesus.

And finally, the church exists to proclaim Jesus to the world. Jesus commissioned His apostles, "Go ye therefore, and teach all nations, baptizing them in the name of the Father, and of the Son, and of the Holy Ghost: teaching them to observe all things whatsoever I have commanded you: and, lo, I am with you alway, even unto the end of the world. Amen" (Matthew 28:19, 20).

Every believer can give a testimony of salvation through Christ, and Jesus also gives a special anointing to some members to be evangelists—bearers of the Good News. The work of bringing others to Jesus, however, is not primarily the work of individuals. It is the work of the body of believers. It takes the assembly to show Jesus to the lost. Individuals give their testimony and some devote much of their time and resources to evangelism, but to bring the knowledge of Jesus to the lost takes more than one member can do. Unbelievers need to be brought into contact with the body of Jesus, the church. They need to see the love, the care, the nurture, the worship, and the ministry of the body of Christ to truly know Jesus and be drawn into faith.

Do I need to be a member of a church to be a Christian?

"But now are they many members, yet but one body. And the eye cannot say unto the hand, I have no need of thee: nor again the head to the feet, I have no need of you" (1 Corinthians 12:20, 21).

God intends believers to function together as an assembly of His people. Many people today think of the church as a building, as a place to go. But the New Testament shows the church as the assembly of those who are saved in Christ.

The assembled believers operate as a body with each member taking his part, each member receiving care, protection, strength, and nurture from the other members. Every member must have his own relationship with God, but God intends that every member experience that relationship in union with the other members of Christ's body. Without the nurturing of the church, a believer will be seriously handicapped and undernourished. Nowhere in the New Testament is a Christian instructed how to live his faith apart from the body of believers.

How do I know what church to join?

This is an excellent question, and it may seem unfortunate that we even need to ask the question. The reality is, however, that not all churches follow Jesus. There are leaders and whole churches that have fallen away from the truth. This has caused some people to give up and conclude that it is hopeless—there are no good churches.

But the very fact that there are imitators tells us there must be genuine believers. Being a good student of the Bible is helpful in making a wise decision about joining with fellow believers in a local church. Following are some Scriptures and evaluating questions you might consider carefully in choosing Christian fellowship:

1. Does the pastor believe the Bible and preach from it? 2 Timothy 4:1-4
2. Do the members love the Lord and do they truly worship Him? John 4:23, 24
3. Are the members serious about following Jesus? Luke 9:23-25

4. Do the members live godly lives? Ephesians 5:3-5

5. Do the members talk honestly to one another about their spiritual progress, and do they offer encouragement and help to fellow members? Ephesians 5:19-21 and Hebrews 10:24, 25

6. Do the members share their faith with unbelievers? Matthew 28:19, 20

Another way to clarify what kind of church to join would be to study Jesus' words to the seven churches in Revelation 2 and 3. In this series of messages, Jesus speaks to each of seven churches and points out to them their strengths and weaknesses. From these seven messages, you might compile a list of characteristics that are important for a church to demonstrate. This could help you to hear directly from Jesus what is important in a church.

In looking for a church, of course, we must not expect to find a perfect church. Though God's children are all in the process of becoming more and more like Jesus, they can and do make mistakes. The important things are that we truly do love and worship Him, that we follow Him as our Lord and Saviour, that we love one another fervently, and that we are serious about bringing the Good News of Jesus to the lost around us.

How does church fellowship contribute to the victorious life?

Again note Ephesians 4:14. "That we henceforth be no more children, tossed to and fro, and carried about with every wind of doctrine, by the sleight of men, and cunning craftiness, whereby they lie in wait to deceive." Note that this is in the context of helping one another achieve spiritual maturity in the body of Christ.

The church blesses members in countless ways. Here are examples:

1. The church provides spiritual instruction to believers.
2. The church warns against spiritual dangers.
3. The church offers a collective wisdom impossible for one member to have by himself.
4. The church gives believers a clearer sense of identity than they have on their own. As members of the church, they are clearly not "of the world."
5. The church offers support and resources for

difficulties in life including loss, sorrow, sickness, temptation, rejection, disability, and loneliness.

6. The church becomes the "family" of believers.
7. The church provides many avenues of ministry, providing opportunities to use one's gifts and resources meaningfully.
8. The church provides channels for using material means for eternal good.
9. The church exercises loving discipline for waywardness and spiritual drift.
10. The church provides many opportunities for lasting and meaningful friendship.
11. The church exposes believers to experiences of divine presence and power as God makes Himself known.
12. In the church, believers meet the loving, living Jesus.

Again, no congregation provides all these blessings perfectly. Sometimes believers have experienced scandalous substitutes instead. But God's plan is that the church—the assembly of the saints—protects members from false ideas and gives those members strength to stand for truth. How easy it is to grow spiritually lopsided apart from the balance of fellow

Christians! What dangers a man exposes himself to when he refuses the shaping and nurture in the assembly of saints! The blessing and benefits of healthy church life cannot be calculated, and believers should commit themselves to being members that make Biblical church life a reality. Jesus said, "Upon this rock I will build my church; and the gates of hell shall not prevail against it" (Matthew 16:18). There is spiritual safety in the assembly of the saints. There is spiritual peril outside of it. Those who want to live victoriously will want to live in union with fellow Christians.

PART III

UNDERSTANDING THE SPIRITUAL BATTLE

"*For we wrestle not against flesh and blood, but against principalities, against powers, against the rulers of the darkness of this world, against spiritual wickedness in high places*" *(Ephesians 6:12).*

Those who would leave the self-life and would live the Christ-life will be opposed. Satan hates those who love Christ. In this section we will explore what the New Testament says about the enemy, his tactics, and God's provision for overcoming him.

THE ENEMY— MURDEROUS DECEIVER

ACCORDING TO JESUS, the devil "was a murderer from the beginning, and abode not in the truth, because there is no truth in him. When he speaketh a lie, he speaketh of his own: for he is a liar, and the father of it" (John 8:44). Jesus also said, "The thief cometh not, but for to steal, and to kill, and to destroy" (John 10:10).

Satan's desire is to destroy, hinder, or wreck in any way he can whatever God does. He hates people. He is intent on our spiritual ruin. Ultimately he wants to send every person he can to destruction. Along the way, he will rob us of dignity, purity, health, and sanity if he can. He delights in rendering people miserable, weak, and hopeless. He takes sadistic pleasure in causing pain and suffering.

Satan is also a deceiver. He operates on lies, trickery, distortion, and treachery. He knows how to present smut and filth in the most alluring packaging. He makes offers only that he might take away. He appears to give and actually strips us of everything he can. He twists the truth but in the twisting makes it appear to be better. Error and doubt and lies are his specialties, and he makes people believe they are being wise to believe what he says and wiser still to persuade others in the same deception. The Apostle Paul wrote, "For such are false apostles, deceitful workers, transforming themselves into the apostles of Christ. And no marvel; for Satan himself is transformed into an angel of light. Therefore it is no great thing if his ministers also be transformed as the ministers of righteousness; whose end shall be according to their works" (2 Corinthians 11:13-15).

What do we know about Satan himself?

WARNING: Some people today have an unhealthy fascination with evil powers. Satan can exploit that and actually draw them into evil through that very fascination. This study is not for those who are fascinated with evil, but for those who abhor it and seek to avoid it.

Jesus said, "I beheld Satan as lightning fall from heaven" (Luke 10:18).

Isaiah the Prophet wrote a powerful rebuke to the proud King of Babylon in words that reflect the pride and destruction of Satan himself. "How art thou fallen from heaven, O Lucifer, son of the morning!

how art thou cut down to the ground, which didst weaken the nations! For thou hast said in thine heart, I will ascend into heaven, I will exalt my throne above the stars of God: I will sit also upon the mount of the congregation, in the sides of the north: I will ascend above the heights of the clouds; I will be like the most High" (Isaiah 14:12-14).

Peter writes about the "angels that sinned," who were cast down to hell (2 Peter 2:4).

As a fallen angel, Satan has great spiritual power. No man or woman is a match for him. All that he was in angelic might is now turned into hellish design, and were it not for the limitations God has placed on him, Satan would use that power to destroy us outright. Satan is a created being, however, and he is not all-powerful. He is not God's exact counterpart. He does not know everything. He does not have the power to do anything he might wish. He cannot be present in all places at once. For this, we can be eternally grateful!

What tactics does Satan use against believers?

Satan's desire is to damage and destroy. From the

Scriptures we know that he uses a variety of methods to achieve his goals. Part of our spiritual alertness is to understand these tactics and take necessary precautions. The Apostle Paul instructed the believers at Corinth in this regard, "lest Satan should get an advantage of us: for we are not ignorant of his devices" (2 Corinthians 2:11). To be forewarned, in other words, is to be forearmed.

Let's look at some of these "devices."

1. Satan plagues believers with temptation.

"Let no man say when he is tempted, I am tempted of God: for God cannot be tempted with evil, neither tempteth he any man: but every man is tempted, when he is drawn away of his own lust, and enticed. Then when lust hath conceived, it bringeth forth sin: and sin, when it is finished, bringeth forth death" *(James 1:13-15).*

These verses tell us that God is not the tempter. They also show us that temptations play on our own desires. We have a desire for food and drink on a physical level. On a deeper level, we want to be loved, we want to be safe, and we want to belong. On a deeper level still, we long for an object of worship—someone (or something) on which to set our devotion. These desires and longings are not wrong in the root sense, but they are the strings Satan plays on to tempt us.

We see this clearly in the temptations of Jesus. Matthew records, "Then was Jesus led up of the Spirit into the wilderness to be tempted of the devil. And when he had fasted forty days and forty nights, he was afterward an hungered. And when the tempter came to him, he said, If thou be the Son of God, command that these stones be made bread" (Matthew 4:1-3).

Jesus was hungry—a legitimate bodily desire. Satan played on Jesus' hunger to try to get Jesus to use His divine power to turn stones into bread. The desire to eat was not wrong. But for Jesus to use His power to prove that He was the Son of God would have been the wrong way to go about eating and the wrong way to show who He was. The Father would have been pleased at this point to have His Son eat, and the Father would have been pleased to have His Son's divine power revealed. But neither the Father nor the Son had any need to prove anything to Satan.

How subtly Satan buries wrong motivations into our eating, into our friendships, into our work, into our play, into our identity, and even into our worship.

Later, he said to Jesus, "All these [kingdoms] will I give thee, if thou wilt fall down and worship me" (v. 9). Jesus was destined to receive those kingdoms, but not in this way.

The subtlety of temptation is that it always touches some part of legitimacy. Food, drink, security, identity, love, worship—these are all part of being human. For all of these things, God has given guidelines for how we satisfy these desires. Temptation is Satan's enticement to ignore God's directions.

By ignoring God's directions and following Satan's suggestions, men and women fall into gluttony, addiction, sloth, immorality, treachery, pride, rivalry, hatred, selfishness, and idolatry. There is no end to the corruptions that result when we listen to the deception of the tempter. And sooner or later those corruptions of legitimate desires will lead to heartache, emptiness, disappointment, misery, and destruction.

Based on the Scriptures we have considered here, we can say that temptation is enticement to—

a. Satisfy legitimate desires for wrong reasons.
b. Ignore God's directions.
c. Seek good things at the wrong time or in the wrong manner.
d. Do things to establish who we are, rather than

trusting God to lead us.

e. Sacrifice greater things for lesser things—as sacrificing honor for money.

As we noted before, Satan is a master deceiver. He likes to make bad things look good. But he also makes good things look awful. He can make it appear that God's directions are unfair—as he did with Eve in the first temptation (Genesis 3). He can make obedience look too difficult to be possible. Or he can make us feel stupid for doing right. Thus, he makes it appear that moral purity is "out-of-date" or "prudish" or "unfair" or "just too difficult." He makes honesty in business appear impractical. He equates truth with harshness or he calls faithfulness and obedience "legalism." In countless ways he twists, distorts, and deceives.

2. Satan uses false teachers who pretend to be from God.

Earlier we noted this verse from Paul's writings: "For Satan himself is transformed into an angel of light. Therefore it is no great thing if his ministers also be transformed as the ministers of righteousness; whose end shall be according to their works"

(2 Corinthians 11:14, 15). Satan is a master of masquerade. Today he deceives many people through "Christian" media. Deceivers speak on "Christian" radio and "Christian" television shows. Deceivers teach in "Christian" colleges. Deceivers perform in "Christian" musical ensembles. Deceivers stand behind pulpits.

How do we know the true from the false?

First, we have the test of God's Word. Paul wrote, "Though we, or an angel from heaven, preach any other gospel unto you than that which we have preached unto you, let him be accursed" (Galatians 1:8). Satan loves to distort the true Gospel. The true Gospel calls people to repent of sin, receive Jesus as their salvation, and follow Him as their Lord. Those who teach another Gospel are deceivers.

Second, a true minister of God will call us away from the world toward God. When Paul urged Timothy to preach the Word of God clearly and fully, he warned, "For the time will come when they will not endure sound doctrine; but after their own lusts shall they heap to themselves teachers, having itching ears; and they shall turn away their ears from the truth, and shall be turned unto fables" (2 Timothy 4:3, 4).

Any teacher or singer who leads people to indulge their desires and ignore God's directions is fulfilling this prophecy. Many religious people today want to hear that they can follow the world, indulge the flesh, feed whatever desires they want in whatever way they want, and still be Christians. In Paul's words, they have "itching ears." That is, they want to hear the things that will ease the discomfort of their consciences and allow them to feel good doing what they want and ignoring God's directions for their lives.

The Apostle John wrote, "Love not the world, neither the things that are in the world. If any man love the world, the love of the Father is not in him. For all that is in the world, the lust of the flesh, and the lust of the eyes, and the pride of life, is not of the Father, but is of the world. And the world passeth away, and the lust thereof: but he that doeth the will of God abideth for ever" (1 John 2:15-17).

There is much in the world that appeals to fleshly desires, and many people live for the weekend when they can eat and drink and party, when they can watch movies that stir their sensual desires, when they can have the kind of "fun" that appeals to whatever desires their bodies have. This is "the lust of the flesh."

There is much in the world that appeals to the desires of our "eyes," that is, to the things we see that make us want more. The advertising world does this constantly, giving us pictures of things to wear, things to play with, things to occupy our time, things that look nice, things we can set up to look at, things that will make us look good to others. As we see all these things, we want them. We desire to have the latest, the "new version," the gadget with the newest features, the hottest fad, the fashion that is now in style, the collectable that is all the rage. When we follow the desires of our eyes, we regularly get what we do not need, we buy new before the old is half used or worn out, and we get more than we need. Consequently, our closets are so full that we cannot possibly wear everything we have. Our drawers we can hardly shut. We box up the excess in storage or take it off to collection places or just throw it away. All because we follow the desires of our eyes—we want whatever we see.

There is also much in the world that appeals to our vanity, or in John's words, "the pride of life." We like for others to look up to us with admiration, to wish they could be like us. Now there is a right place for being admired (for our character, for example), just as there is a right place for satisfying the needs of the body and for buying the things we need for daily living. But the pride of life is based on things that are superficial to who we really are.

In the world, people are admired for their wealth, for their physical appearance, for their clothes, for their position in life, for their educational background, for the size of their house, for the luxuries they have in and around their house, for the vacations they can take, for the kind of car or truck they drive, for their recreational vehicles, for the unique possessions they can boast of. . . . And yet, a man or woman may have all of these things and be a scoundrel, be very difficult to live with, and be a very miserable person. He can boast of much and be greatly admired, but he is a man of the world. She can be the model every lady in town wants to look like and act like and talk like, but she is a woman of the world.

"Love not the world," John writes. Many religious leaders today live the worldly life themselves and preach a message that scratches the ears of worldly-minded people. Some teach that God gives you whatever you desire, that it is God's will for you to be materially wealthy and have whatever you want. Satan uses this message to deceive people into disregarding the earthly mission God has given to His people and outright disobeying many of God's instructions.

"Dearly beloved, I beseech you as strangers and pilgrims, abstain from fleshly lusts, which war against the soul" (1 Peter 2:11).

"And having food and raiment let us be therewith content. For the love of money is the root of all evil: which while some coveted after, they have erred from the faith, and pierced themselves through with many sorrows" (1 Timothy 6:8, 10).

"Lay not up for yourselves treasures upon earth, where moth and rust doth corrupt, and where thieves break through and steal: but lay up for yourselves treasures in heaven, where neither moth nor rust doth corrupt, and where thieves do not break through nor steal: for where your treasure is, there will your heart be also" (Matthew 6:19-21).

"Whose adorning let it not be that outward adorning of plaiting the hair, and of wearing of gold, or of putting on of apparel; but let it be the hidden man of the heart, in that which is not corruptible, even the ornament of a meek and quiet spirit, which is in the sight of God of great price" (1 Peter 3:3, 4).

We must beware of listening to voices that tell us it

is all right to do what God's Word forbids.

3. Satan uses tactics of intimidation.

"Be sober, be vigilant; because your adversary the devil, as a roaring lion, walketh about, seeking whom he may devour: whom resist stedfast in the faith" (1 Peter 5:8, 9).

Believers are secure in Christ. Of course, they may choose to depart from Him, and we know that apart from Christ, there is no security. But by abiding in Christ, they are safe. Christ has overcome Satan and stripped him of his power. Nothing Satan does or says can destroy the security we have in Jesus. "For I am persuaded, that neither death, nor life, nor angels, nor principalities, nor powers, nor things present, nor things to come, nor height, nor depth, nor any other creature, shall be able to separate us from the love of God, which is in Christ Jesus our Lord" (Romans 8:38, 39).

In spite of this reality, Satan attacks believers as though he could overcome them. He would love to have us doubt our security in Christ. Like a roaring lion, he can appear dreadful, powerful, and unstoppable. In his intimidation, he may hurl accusations at believers, either about their present blunders or their past sins. He may weigh on believers as a heavy influence of discouragement or doubt or fear. He may bring dreadful things to their mind, ideas they do not wish to think about. He may cast shadows over every promise in the Bible. By these tactics he seeks to shake believers from their faith and cause them to stumble.

These are tactics of intimidation. Satan "roars" as a lion in order to strike fear, doubt, and discouragement into the hearts of believers. If we listen to his accusations about us, his attacks on the promises of God and the character of God, or his boastful display of his own accomplishments, we will get our eyes off God. And in that loss of focus, we may fall. God's Word tells us to resist this roaring lion by faith. We have the assurance that "God hath not given us the spirit of fear; but of power, and of love, and of a sound mind" (2 Timothy 1:7).

Faith calls us to . . .

a. Believe what God has said.

b. Expect/wait on what God has promised.

c. Trust God's good purposes in our lives.

d. Refuse to listen to the voice of Satan, whether he speaks loudly or softly.

4. Satan uses affliction.

The Apostle Paul wrote, "There was given to me a thorn in the flesh, the messenger of Satan to buffet me, lest I should be exalted above measure" (2 Corinthians 12:7).

Satan attacked Job with the loss of all his possessions, including his children. When Job would not be moved by this, Satan claimed Job would buckle under physical suffering. "So went Satan forth from the presence of the Lord, and smote Job with sore boils from the sole of his foot unto his crown" (Job 2:7).

When temptation doesn't work, when deception doesn't work, when intimidation doesn't work, Satan may resort to affliction. Severe trials, losses, grief, persecution, sickness, and pain wear on the believer. If the suffering is long, resistance tends to break down. Believers begin to question God. Why me, God? Where are You? What are You doing to me? Where are Your promises? What good is it doing me to be a Christian?

Both Job and Paul struggled with the physical attacks they received at the hand of Satan. Both also learned that God is faithful and good no matter what experiences we go through in this life. Both learned to trust God more fully. Whenever God allows Satan to "buffet" His children, He always places a limit, He always supplies special grace, and He always has purposes for what He is allowing. Eventually, the very thing Satan does against us is used by God to bring about better things in our experience.

God truly does care about His children. He is always deeply concerned for them when they are in the fires of affliction. He is able to accomplish infinitely more good than Satan can inflict evil—at the same time, and using those very afflictions. But believers sometimes lose sight of this. And Satan, even when he knows he cannot ultimately overcome true believers, seems to enjoy watching them suffer temporarily. Affliction is one of his hate tactics on those specially loved of God.

These are the subtle workings of Satan. We turn now to the resources available to the believer.

THE CHRISTIAN'S ARMOR— EFFECTIVE SPIRITUAL WEAPONS

"PUT ON THE WHOLE ARMOUR OF GOD, that ye may be able to stand against the wiles of the devil. For we

wrestle not against flesh and blood, but against principalities, against powers, against the rulers of the darkness of this world, against spiritual wickedness in high places" (Ephesians 6:11, 12).

In the spiritual battle, we need spiritual armor. The Apostle Paul uses an extended analogy of a soldier's armor to show us how to stand against our spiritual enemy. We will examine each of these, recognizing they are analogies that do not tell us everything about spiritual victory, but that they give us vital information.

How can we stand against the enemy?

"My brethren, be strong in the Lord, and in the power of his might" (Ephesians 6:10). The most fundamental reality of the spiritual battle is that Christ is the victor over Satan. We do not stand a chance apart from Christ. He has conquered Satan, and He has conquered him decisively. The Scriptures leave us with no doubt on this point.

"Having disarmed principalities and powers, He made a public spectacle of them, triumphing over them in it" (Colossians 2:15, NKJV).

"Forasmuch then as the children are partakers of

flesh and blood, he also himself likewise took part of the same; that through death he might destroy him that had the power of death, that is, the devil; and deliver them who through fear of death were all their lifetime subject to bondage" (Hebrews 2:14, 15).

"For this purpose the Son of God was manifested, that he might destroy the works of the devil" (1 John 3:8).

Satan is a defeated foe. When Jesus was crucified, it appeared that the devil had gained a victory. But three days after Jesus' death on the cross, He rose from the dead. He "tasted death," the worst Satan could do, exactly in order to break that stronghold of evil. Death had no power over Jesus. Peter says, "It was not possible that he should be holden of it!" (Acts 2:24). Jesus said, "I am the resurrection, and the life" (John 11:25). By rising from the dead, Jesus shattered the power of the devil. He made a "public spectacle" of His victory over Satan.

Furthermore, when Jesus died, He died for us. His death was in our behalf. His blood was given to atone for our sins. Those who believe in Jesus as their Saviour, therefore, are forgiven by God and are rescued from the destruction awaiting all who have followed Satan in his rebellion against God.

The cross, then, was a decisive victory over Satan. Through the cross, Jesus broke the power of death. He secured the forgiveness of our sins. And He defeated our worst enemy.

All this truth about Jesus' victory over Satan is embedded in Paul's instruction to "be strong in the Lord, and in the power of his might" (Ephesians 6:10). We are no match for Satan, but Satan is no match for Jesus. We must stand against the devil in the strength of Jesus, in total union with Him. When we walk with Jesus, we are safe. When we walk with Jesus, the enemy has no weapon that can destroy us. John writes, "We know that anyone born of God does not continue to sin; the one who was born of God [Jesus] keeps him safe, and the evil one does not touch him" (1 John 5:18, NIV).

This does not mean, of course, that we never suffer loss or pain, or that we have no trouble. As we noted earlier, God allows His children to suffer at times, but always with restrictions, always with an ample supply of grace, and always according to His good purposes.

When we face the evil one—whether his temptations or his attacks—we need to stand firm in our position in Christ. Spiritually, we are united with Jesus. He lives in us, and our life is in Him. We speak in His name, we act in His name, we stand in His name, we pray in His name, and we go forward in His name.

We have no power against the enemy apart from the power of Christ. Without our spiritual union with Jesus, we are "toast." This is the most fundamental dimension to spiritual victory. We cannot stand against the devil through determination, through learning the proper formula to repeat to him, by exercising greater effort, or even by quoting Scripture (though these things may have their place). We stand against the devil through Christ. Jesus is a living, real person, and we must know Him. We must walk with Him daily. Without Him, we cannot stand. With Him, we cannot be destroyed.

Jesus gives us spiritual protection. This is the meaning of the spiritual armor Paul discusses in Ephesians 6. As we walk with Jesus, we come to know the truth and align our lives with the truth. As we walk with Him, we learn what is right and we practice doing what is right. As we walk with Him, we testify to the truth and power of the Good News of Jesus, our faith deepens, we experience the saving work of God, and we exercise ourselves in the Word of God. Each of these dimensions of our experience with Jesus becomes a means of protection against the enemy of our souls. Paul describes these dimensions of spiritual protection figuratively as pieces of our armor—the "belt of truth," the "breastplate of right-eousness," the "boots of the Gospel of peace," the "shield of faith," the "helmet of salvation," and the "sword of God's Word."

These "pieces of armor" should not be viewed as independent things we do or say or acquire to over-come temptation, nor are they spiritual "tactics." Rather, they are intertwined dimensions of living in union with Jesus. So as we consider these pieces of armor, keep in mind that they are protections we have coming from the person and presence of Jesus in our lives. They are not seven distinct or indepen-dent methods of protecting ourselves.

To stand against the enemy:

1. We need the belt of truth.

Those who live with Jesus interact with the Truth. He is the truth, according to His own words: "I am the way, the truth, and the life" (John 14:6). When we walk with Jesus, we walk with the One who embodies all truth—He knows the truth, He speaks the truth, He lives the truth, and He imparts the truth because He is the truth. Our interaction with Jesus is protection for us in the spiritual warfare because, as we noted earlier, Satan's primary weapon against us is deception.

Satan questions the truth. He distorts and twists the truth. He tells lies and half-truths. He makes accusations and insinuations against God, against God's Word, and against God's people.

We must know the truth—we must protect our vital organs, as it were—with the belt of truth.

This protection of truth is more than knowing things that are true. A drunkard may know that it is unhealthy to get drunk. He may know that the money he spends for drink he needs for other things. He may know that his drinking is ruining his relationships and endangering his job. He may know that it is unwise to go to a bar because he will spend his money, get drunk, feel terrible, and get into trouble. Knowing those things that are true still doesn't protect him from doing it all over again. Even knowing things that are true, the drunkard is still losing the war over his soul.

Knowing the truth involves knowing the Person, the One who is the Truth.

Putting on the belt of truth also involves owning the truth. That is, it means taking the truth into one's life and becoming true.

One of the most ironic statements in the Bible is found in the story of Joseph and his brothers. They had hated him, sold him into slavery, and then fabricated a story about having found Joseph's clothing—torn and bloody. And so, Jacob believed Joseph was dead while Joseph served as a slave in Egypt. Years later, after Joseph had suffered imprisonment for refusing to compromise his character and was then put into the second highest ruling position in the land, Joseph one day found his brothers standing before him. Not knowing who they were talking to, they said, "We are true men!" (Genesis 42:11). Imagine what went through Joseph's mind hearing that declaration.

Truth is more than something we know. It needs to be something we are. Truth goes beyond knowing what is true to being true. Truth is doing what is right even when it is difficult, even when no one is looking, even when it results in loss and suffering.

Truth is a way of being.

We become true men and women as we live in union with Jesus. He fills us with Himself, teaching us what is true and giving us the courage and character to be true in all situations. This is what it means to wear the belt of truth. To know the truth and be true to the One we know is protection against the devil. The enemy is frustrated when indeed we are "true men."

The opposite is also true. When we are not true to what we know, when we compromise character, when we say one thing and do another, when we are loving one day and treacherous the next, we are not able to stand against the enemy. He has us in exactly the place he wants us. We are playing his game, and he will win.

Our Father in heaven, forgive our duplicity and make us true. We implore You to fill us with the life of Your Son, the only One who was perfectly true! Where we fail, where we sin, where we compromise, give us at least the integrity to say what is true—that we are wretched and sinful, and that we need to be forgiven, cleansed, and restored to the likeness of Your Son. We ask

You to enable us to embrace the truth in our being, to make our living one with our knowing. Grant us true hearts and then true words and true actions. Lord Jesus, You who are the Truth, live Your life in us. Defend us against the deceptions of the enemy, against the deceptions of sin, and against the deceptions of the self-life. Help us pull the belt of truth around the Treasure in our innermost being, and protect us for Your name's sake. Amen.

2. We need the breastplate of righteousness.

Our root problem is that we are sinful. According to God's judgment, "There is none righteous, no, not one" (Romans 3:10). Jesus died to forgive us for our sins, but that is not all He intends to do. He also intends to make us righteous. He does this in two ways.

First, He counts our faith as righteousness. We saw earlier that the Bible calls this "justification." That is, when we believe in Jesus, our faith is credited to us as righteousness. This righteousness is possible, of course, because of what Jesus did in our behalf. As Paul said, we are "justified by his blood" (Romans 5:9). In itself, faith could not rightly be called righteousness, but faith in Jesus (because of who He is and because of what He did for us) is rightly called righteousness.

We see again that the armor of the believer is inseparable from the person of Jesus. Our ability to stand in the spiritual battle against the devil depends on who Jesus is to us. In this case, we were sinners and sentenced to death. He was perfectly righteous and died for us. We believe in Him, and our faith in Him is credited to us as righteousness. This righteousness functions as a "breastplate" to protect us from the attacks of Satan.

The devil would love to accuse us. But the Bible says, "There is therefore now no condemnation to them which are in Christ Jesus, who walk not after the flesh, but after the Spirit" (Romans 8:1). Furthermore, Paul asks, not arrogantly, but with total confidence, "Who shall lay any thing to the charge of God's elect? It is God that justifieth" (8:33). In other words, not one of Satan's accusations can stick against those who believe in Jesus because the declaration that we are righteous comes from the mouth of God Himself. "Who is he that condemneth? It is Christ that died, yea rather, that is risen again, who is even at the right hand of God, who also maketh intercession for us" (v. 34). The answer to the question is, "No one!" Because Jesus died for us and because He stands at the right hand of God speaking in our behalf, no one can bring a condemning indictment against a true believer.

The righteousness of justification protects us.

But believers have more than imputed righteousness. The effect of faith is not only that we are declared righteous, but that we are made righteous. The Gospel of Christ, Paul says, reveals a righteousness that is "from faith to faith" and results in living that faith. "For therein is the righteousness of God revealed from faith to faith: as it is written, The just shall live by faith" (Romans 1:17).

John writes, "Little children, let no man deceive you: he that doeth righteousness is righteous, even as he [Jesus] is righteous" (1 John 3:7). And a few verses later he makes righteousness of life one defining difference between believers and unbelievers. "In this the children of God are manifest, and the children of the devil: whosoever doeth not righteousness is not of God, neither he that loveth not his brother" (v. 10). One effect of placing our faith in Jesus is a change in heart that results in a change of life.

This brings into focus an important aside here:

"Christianity" that offers peace and pardon and a home in heaven with no change in one's way of living is a false Christianity. If there is no difference in the lifestyle, the ethics, and the morality of believers, and the lifestyle, ethics, and morality of unbelievers, there has been no salvation. Jesus does not save people to enable them to go on sinning. In the words of the angel to Joseph, "Thou shalt call his name JESUS [deliverer]: for he shall save his people from their sins" (Matthew 1:21).

Faith results in righteous living. In Biblical understanding, there is no separation between faith and obedience—those who believe act accordingly; those who do not believe also act accordingly. Faith results in doing what God says; unbelief results in ignoring what God says and doing what I want to do.

As we noted earlier, this does not mean that a believer lives perfectly or that he never sins. It simply means that when we place our faith in Jesus, we turn from a life of sin to a life of righteousness. Our intent is to do what Jesus says. There is an immediate change in behavior—away from doing what is sinful toward doing what is right—and this results in a lifelong growth into the image of Jesus.

This righteousness of life is not the product of our

101

own effort—though it does take effort on our part. Rather, it is the result of Jesus living in us, of us immersing our minds in Him, and of us yielding our wills and our desires to His will and His desire. Jesus in us—speaking, urging, energizing, and directing us—produces this changed way of living. We see the results, then, as Jesus saving us from sin and Jesus producing good works in us. We are not saved by these works, but we are saved to do these righteous works. "For by grace are ye saved through faith; and that not of yourselves: it is the gift of God: not of works, lest any man should boast. For we are his workmanship, created in Christ Jesus unto good works, which God hath before ordained that we should walk in them" (Ephesians 2:8-10).

This righteousness of life resulting from living in spiritual union with Jesus is spiritual protection against the enemy. The believer who refuses to do what the enemy suggests, who instead receives his instructions for living from Jesus, and who, as a result, does what is right is protected from all sorts of spiritual snares. His exercise in doing right increases his spiritual understanding, and he is not as easily hoodwinked by sin. His righteousness protects him from the crippling effects of shame, from relational strain, and from the discouragement of failure. The practice of doing right also increases spiritual strength. As the songwriter says, "Each victory will help you/ Some other to win!"

Ironically, the very blessings and protections of righteous living also carry a subtle snare. When we develop practices of doing right through the presence and life of Jesus, our focus may stray from Jesus to ourselves. We may come to think of right living as the result of our own understanding, our own strength, and our own goodness. We can shift from seeing ourselves as utterly dependent on Jesus to taking personal pride in the things Jesus has done in us and through us. And then we fall.

Not one day, not one temptation, not one responsibility may we take on without the Lord Jesus. Our truly good works are never our own. They are always the result of Jesus living in us. They are the "fruit" of the spiritual nutrients coming from the divine life of Jesus. If we are truly loving to others, if we are patient and kind, if we give sacrificially, if we help the weak, if we encourage the disheartened, even if we give a cup of cold water—all is to be done from the life of Jesus in us. He is the eternal fountain of righteousness, pouring forth from our lives.

And such righteous living is protection against the designs of Satan.

Our Father, we thank You for the righteousness of Your Son Jesus. We thank You that You count us righteous as we place our faith in Him. What an eternal wonder that we could be called righteous in Your sight—You, before whose holiness even the angels bow in unutterable reverence! We thank You that You do not leave us in our sin, but that You call us to live right, think right, speak right, and do right. We pray that You would deliver us from evil, that You would purge us of our ways, and that You would grant us power to walk in Your ways. We pray that when we do right, we would always do so with humble awareness that it is You who works in us both to will and to do Your good pleasure. Protect us from the evil designs of the enemy for Your glory, and make us a praise to You in righteousness. Amen.

3. We need the boots of the Gospel

Having your "feet shod with the preparation of the gospel of peace" (Ephesians 6:15). "How beautiful are the feet of them that preach the gospel of peace, and bring glad tidings of good things!" (Romans 10:15). Sharing the Good News of Jesus is spiritual protection against the enemy.

For one thing, when we share the Good News of Jesus, whether with individuals or with groups, we are fulfilling an ongoing mission Jesus gave to His disciples. "All power is given unto me in heaven and in earth. Go ye therefore, and teach all nations, baptizing them in the name of the Father, and of the Son, and of the Holy Ghost: teaching them to observe all things whatsoever I have commanded you: and, lo, I am with you alway even unto the end of the world. Amen" (Matthew 28:18-20).

Jesus gave us the mission to tell others about Him. It is in this mission that He promises us His presence. Although we often think this means we must go somewhere beyond where we are presently (some foreign country), and although going to foreign countries is included here, this is not the focus of the mission. The Greek verb tense suggests, "Going therefore . . ." That is, "In your going" or "As you go" or "Wherever you go." The mission is to tell. We are to tell others about Jesus wherever we go.

How do we do this?

Sometimes we make this more complicated in our

minds than it really is. To share the Gospel with others is simply to talk about who Jesus is. The easiest way to do this is to be ready at any time to tell others what He means to us and what He has done for us. The "personal testimony" can be in the form of thanks, praise, or stories about guidance He gives, about answers to prayer, or simply about the wonder of being His. The best place to start is with fellow believers. The first years of the early church were spent mostly in gatherings to speak and hear about Jesus. As others heard about this secondhand, they came to the gatherings to hear it firsthand. Then later, through the opposition the church received, "they were all scattered abroad throughout the regions of Judaea and Samaria," and consequently, "they that were scattered abroad went every where preaching the word" (Acts 8:1, 4).

The believer needs to be ready to tell his fellow believers what Jesus is saying to him—words of instruction. The believer needs to tell what Jesus has done and is doing for him—forgiving him, cleansing him, strengthening him, and answering his prayers. The believer needs to tell what Jesus means to him—He is precious, He is powerful, He is compassionate, etc. The believer needs to review what Jesus

106

did in His life on earth—how He "went about doing good, and healing all that were oppressed of the devil" (Peter's testimony in Acts 10:38).

Talking about Jesus typically brings us into more opposition from the enemy because Satan hates Jesus and those who are devoted to Him. But the wonderful reality is that this also brings us into greater spiritual protection as well. Jesus is with those who stand up for Him. Whatever opposition they face from the devil and evil people is turned by the power of Jesus into even more powerful revelations of who He is and greater advancement against enemy territory.

In the Book of Acts, this is illustrated over and over. We noted already that the persecution of the believers in Jerusalem served to scatter them, which no doubt felt uncomfortable to them but which resulted in spreading the Gospel to surrounding areas. When Paul and Silas were beaten and thrown into jail for sharing the Gospel, God sent an earthquake that resulted in Paul and Silas's release, the conversion of the jailer and his family, a public display of the power of Jesus, and even the higher officials wanting to pacify these servants of Jesus and downplay their former opposition.

Thus, being ready to share the Gospel—having our "boots on" at all times—does not mean we will never suffer. But it secures the presence of Jesus to turn opposition into advancement.

O Father, we thank You for the glorious plan for our salvation through Your Son Jesus. This is the best news the world has ever heard. It is Your grand story! Do Your work of redemption in our lives, so we can testify of what Jesus has done for us personally. Give us a readiness always to share the Good News with those we live with, those we worship with, those we work with, those we visit with, those we meet casually, and those we meet formally. We want to keep our boots on at all times. Teach us to speak at the right time, to the right people, with the right words, in the right tones—make the Gospel beautiful coming from our lips and powerful in the ears of those who hear. Amen.

4. We need the shield of faith.

Faith in Jesus is an effective shield against sin, against the devil, and against the anti-God world system. "And this is the victory that overcometh the world, even our faith" (1 John 5:4).

We need to bring into focus immediately that faith is no better than its object. In a postmodern society, we are told that all faith is equal, that it doesn't really matter what we believe. This understanding of faith for faith's sake is supposed to be unoffensive to everyone. And it is likewise false.

We would never follow such foolishness in other areas of life. Imagine someone telling you, "Any route will take you to New York. Just so you are on a road—that is the important thing." Or even more consequential, "Trust anyone with your money (or your health or your vehicle). The important thing is that you trust the person. It really doesn't matter what kind of person you are trusting." As someone once said, "A weak faith in a strong plank will get you safely across the stream, but a strong faith in a rotten plank will land you in the middle of it."

The object of our faith is of utmost importance! Our faith—the faith that saves and the faith that protects against the enemy—is in Jesus. We trust Him fully. As Paul said, "I know whom I have believed, and am persuaded that he is able to keep that which I have committed unto him against that day" (1 Timothy 1:12).

A firm faith in Jesus really does protect us from the enemy. Faith serves as a shield against temptation, against doubts, against disobedience, against discouragement and despair. When we trust God—when we have settled it in our hearts that God is all He declares Himself to be—we have a solid base to say no to sin. No matter how attractive sin appears to be, we know it is wrong, and we say no by faith. We also have a clear answer to the doubts and insinuations of the enemy. No matter how skillfully he may argue that God is unfair or unclear or uncaring, and no matter how our circumstances may seem at the moment to correspond to Satan's arguments, we know that God is good, God is right, and God is love. We have anchored our souls on the truth of God, and we will not listen to the suggestions of the enemy.

Such faith is a shield. We are kept from believing Satan's lies. We are kept from acting foolishly according to our feelings in the moment. We are kept from living according to our own understanding.

Our faith is in a Person. It is not first "what" we believe that counts most but "in whom" we believe. Certainly, we believe truths. We believe it is wrong to steal and kill and cheat. We believe it is right to be kind, to share with those in need, and to be faithful to our word. But faith is not primarily a list of do's and don'ts. Faith is not our "statement" or our creed. Faith is a settled trust in God. "But without faith it is impossible to please him: for he that cometh to God must believe that he is, and that he is a rewarder of them that diligently seek him" (Hebrews 11:6).

We trust who God is—fully and completely. And because we believe in Him, we believe what He says. We trust what He does. We do not question what He allows, even though at the time we may be puzzled or confused. We know that it is exactly because we do not fully understand that we need to fully trust.

Those who believe in God find their faith rewarded over and over. Joseph did not understand why God allowed him to be sold as a slave, to be lied about, and to be cast into prison. Job did not understand why God allowed all his possessions to be destroyed, his family to perish, and his health to fail. Naomi did not understand why God allowed her husband and her two sons to die in a foreign land. Daniel did not understand why God allowed the king to throw him to the lions. Paul did not at first understand why God allowed him to be "buffeted" by the devil. But each of these men and women

111

trusted God, and by their faith, they were kept from disobedience and despair. By their faith, they rose above their circumstances and experienced the work of God in their lives.

What is true for difficulty is also true for blessings. Abraham did not fully understand why God gave him a son in his old age. The Israelites did not fully understand why God brought them out of Egypt and gave them the land of Canaan. Esther did not fully understand why she was made queen of Persia, nor did Nehemiah understand why he was the king's cupbearer. But in each of these situations, God called His people to believe in Him, to trust that their blessings had purposes beyond their immediate pleasure or personal welfare. As they lived by that faith, they were delivered from the snares of wealth and prosperity, and they became significant in furthering the purposes of God on earth.

Faith in God is a shield. It is protection against discouragement and despair, against doubt and disobedience, as well as against pride and selfish indulgence. When we believe God, our eyes are on Him. We know that He made us. We know that He has the right to guide us. We know that we have the privilege of being His children and the responsibility of following His directions. As we live that faith, we are kept from the designs of the enemy.

O Father, our eyes are so easily blinded to who You really are. Open the eyes of our heart. Help us to believe in You, to believe everything You say, to affirm everything You do, and to trust everything You allow. Give us grace and resolve to live our faith. Shield us from sin, from deception, and from unbelief. When times are confusing and the light of our understanding grows dim, enable us to believe in You. When we experience blessing and comfort, help us not to forget You are the giver of all good gifts. Shield us from the onslaughts of Satan as well as from his subtle suggestions and lies. We believe in You; help our unbelief! Amen.

5. We need the helmet of salvation

God's children are protected from the enemy by exercising a settled confidence in what God has promised. God has forgiven us, and God is presently delivering us from the designs of the enemy. This calls for faith. But God has also promised in the end to cast down Satan permanently and to take His children to be with Him forever. In Scriptural terminology, this is the "hope of salvation." It is what we look forward to based on the clear and sure promises of God.

The hope of believers is protection against sin and Satan. When we hold this hope firmly in our hearts, we are willing to suffer difficulties now because we have something better in the future. We are willing to have little in this world's goods because we have been promised "an inheritance incorruptible, and undefiled, and that fadeth not away, reserved in heaven for you" (1 Peter 1:4). We accept injustice, plunder, slander, and suffering in this life for the glories promised to us in the world to come. Our hope keeps us from despair.

Some people place the "hope of salvation" on the same level as the uncertain expectations we have in this life. We "hope" it will be a nice day tomorrow. We hope we can do this or go there. We hope we will have enough money to pay the bills. But all these things, of course, are not sure—many things could dash our expectations. But the hope of the believer is not to be reduced to this level of uncertainty. We are uncertain about things in this life because we are limited and frail and fallible. But what God has promised, we have the assurance He is able to fulfill. Because our expectation is in God, we have full assurance. There need be no uncertainty or doubt about the hope of our salvation. It is called "hope" because we have not fully received it, not because it is in question.

The writer to the Hebrews makes this abundantly clear. "Because God wanted to make the unchanging nature of his purpose very clear to the heirs of what was promised, he confirmed it with an oath. God did this so that, by two unchangeable things in which it is impossible for God to lie, we who have fled to take hold of the hope offered to us may be greatly encouraged" (Hebrews 6:17, 18, NIV). In other words, God wanted so much to assure us of the certainty of what He promised that He took an oath—totally unnecessary, but absolutely convincing. So then, the writer continues, "We have this hope as an anchor for the soul, firm and secure" (v. 19).

Our salvation is not fully accomplished—though we are being saved, the completed work is still to come—but the provisions are fully in place. Our expectation in what God has promised to do guards and protects us. As Paul wrote elsewhere, we are to wear the "helmet, the hope of salvation"

(1 Thessalonians 5:8) as protection against the enemy.

Our hope of salvation is again fully bound up in the Person of Jesus. It was His death and resurrection that secured the promises of God for our deliverance from sin. Jesus defeated Satan and sealed his doom. Jesus stands now in our behalf at the right hand of the Father. Jesus has sealed (stamped as His own) those who believe in Him in this age of grace. And Jesus stands ready for the command of the Father to consummate the ages, to gather together those of all eras and all nations in all places who believe in Him. In Christ, all the promises of God to us are secured. The hope of salvation, by which we refuse to give up, by which we suffer now, even gladly, rests in Jesus—who He is, what He has done for us, and what God has promised yet to do for us because of Him.

Because of Jesus, Paul spoke in "no uncertain terms" to the Corinthians about the promises of God. In his own words, "As God is true, our word toward you was not yea and nay. For the Son of God, Jesus Christ, who was preached among you by us, even by me and Silvanus and Timotheus, was not yea and nay, but in him was yea. For all the promises of God in him are yea, and in him Amen, unto the glory of

God by us" (2 Corinthians 1:18-20).

O Father, Your saving work is grand beyond our comprehension, and what You have promised to those who believe in Your Son passes all reason or thought. You have promised to end the reign of sin, to bring this present world to destruction, to throw down the strongholds of the enemy, to usher in the reign of righteousness, to create new heavens and a new earth, and to give us a home with You for eternity. Hallelujah to You forever! Protect our heads and our hearts with this hope! We rest in what You have said. We expect You to do what You have promised. We believe that You will bring our salvation to completion through Your Son. Even so, come, Lord Jesus! Amen.

6. We need the "sword of the Spirit, which is the word of God."

In the day-to-day battle against the lies, mockery, accusations, temptations, and harassment of the enemy, we have a very practical weapon—God's Word. The imagery used here, is that we wield the Word of God like a sword, with the unction of the

117

Holy Spirit, to combat the enemy. In plain language, this means we must know what God has said in His Word. It means that as we face temptations, we say no to the offers of Satan and the world by recalling what God has said in His Word, repeating that Word to ourselves and to the enemy as need be, and ordering our lives by God's directions rather than the enemy's suggestions.

Jesus demonstrated this use of Scripture in His temptations. When Satan suggested that Jesus make the stones into bread, Jesus said, "It is written, Man shall not live by bread alone, but by every word that proceedeth out of the mouth of God" (Matthew 4:4). When Satan suggested that Jesus should throw Himself down from the temple (even quoting Scripture—misinterpreted—to make his point), Jesus promptly replied, "It is written again, Thou shalt not tempt the Lord thy God" (v. 7). And when Satan offered Jesus all the kingdoms of the world if He would but worship him, Jesus said, "It is written, Thou shalt worship the Lord thy God, and him only shalt thou serve" (v. 10).

We must not conclude that simply quoting a Bible verse gains every victory, but on the other hand, we must not minimize the power of the Word of God in the spiritual battle. Much of the spiritual conflict through the ages has been focused on whether people will believe and follow what God has said or believe and follow the contrary things Satan says. Believers equip themselves to stand against the enemy as they absorb the Word of God by faith. Reading God's Word, hearing God's Word, memorizing God's Word, meditating on God's Word, trusting God's Word, quoting God's Word, and obeying God's Word—all these are involved in our Spirit-directed offensive against the devil.

Using another analogy, Peter urges us, "As newborn babes, desire the sincere milk of the word, that ye may grow thereby" (1 Peter 2:2). Many young Christians have testified that God gave them an insatiable desire to read the Bible in their early experience as believers. This gives the Spirit of God much to work with in our spiritual development and in our struggle against sin. As we face temptations, doubts, trials, opposition, and the need to explain to friends and family what God has done for us, having the Word of God in our hearts is invaluable. The Holy Spirit prompts us with promises, commands, principles, and powerful truths. As we take in the Scriptures, we hear His voice regularly speaking to our hearts the pure Word of God.

The Word of God is also protection against the "winds of doctrine" that are continually blowing across the land. Spiritual "fads" commonly sweep through the religious community—first it is stories about angels, then it is having certain ecstatic experiences, then it is praying in certain phraseology, then it is meditating in solitude, then it is the power of praising God in certain ways, then it is the spiritual disciplines, then it is attending a seminar, then it is joining a small group. All of these things may have their legitimate place. What often happens, however, is that the "in thing" is given such emphasis and prominence and attended with such promises and expectations that people are sidetracked from living for Jesus.

Furthermore, these kinds of emphases sometimes are used as a cover for disobedience. People may join a spiritual movement that is heralded as an "awakening" and at the same time be involved in such sins as divorce and remarriage, homosexual relationships, self-centered living, oppression of the poor, and material accumulation. This is not new. Jude warned against those who "change the grace of our God into a license for immorality" (v. 4, NIV).

How we need the "Spirit's sword" to stand faithfully in our day!

O Father, thank You for Your eternal Word. Thank You for those who recorded Your Word for us. Thank You for those who passed it down faithfully through the ages. Thank You for those who have translated it into our language. Thank You that Your Word is true, powerful, and relevant in every age and culture. Enable us to absorb Your Word into our hearts. Write it on our minds. Speak Your Word into our lives when we face temptation, when we need direction, and when we are confused with conflicting voices in the world around us. Grant us wisdom to order our lives in such a way that we have time to read Your Word, meditate on it, study it, and take it into our lives. Enable us to use Your Word effectively when speaking to others. We confess with all our hearts that Your Word is true. We rest our lives and hopes on it for time and for eternity. Amen.

7. Finally, we need to pray.

Prayer is not listed as a piece of "armor" or as a

spiritual "weapon," but Paul concludes this extended discussion on spiritual battle with a call to prayer. "Praying always with all prayer and supplication in the Spirit, and watching thereunto with all perseverance and supplication for all saints" (Ephesians 6:18).

Notice here, we are to pray "in the Spirit." When we pray, we enter the spiritual realm—the realm where God is, where angels dwell, where we can receive spiritual direction, but also a realm where the enemy is, where the spiritual battle rages, and where demons continually attack and torment and plot their wicked designs.

To pray in the Spirit means we pray in union with the Spirit of God. We meditate on His intentions. We mesh our own hearts with His will. We implore God to bring about the things that accomplish His designs. And we stand against the designs of the enemy. We resist his will in our own lives and in the lives of others. We pray God to frustrate the enemy, to stop his progress, to throw back upon him his own plans so that what the enemy does against God's people turns actually to the advantage of God's people.

To pray in the Spirit takes us beyond our own interests. We pray heart to heart with God for His purposes to be accomplished on the earth. As these extend beyond our own understanding, we sometimes halt in prayer—our knowledge is limited; we don't know what is best though we desire it. But we are encouraged here by Paul's words to the Romans: "Likewise the Spirit also helpeth our infirmities: for we know not what we should pray for as we ought: but the Spirit itself maketh intercession for us with groanings which cannot be uttered" (Romans 8:26).

Paul's guidance in Ephesians 6 is not only that we pray in the Spirit, but that we pray *"for all saints."* Our prayers are to be for the people of God. We pray for their protection. We pray that their strength will be increased. We pray that their understanding in God will continually grow, solidifying their commitments to God and fortifying their hearts against sin. We pray for their eternal good. We pray they will not give up or lose heart. We pray that their hearts will be purified and that their testimony in the world will be clear.

Many of our prayer meetings today are focused on the lost—people who need to receive Jesus. It is not wrong to pray for the unsaved. But Paul teaches us by word and example that much prayer should be focused on believers. They are under attack from

Satan. They are living in enemy territory. And they need support.

Many of Paul's prayers for believers were for their spiritual understanding. In the hurry of daily living, in the press of duties, in the constant going of sights and sounds and tangible realities, we easily lose sight of things spiritual. We can forget that God is. We can lose sight of His promises. Our spiritual commitments—made in such clarity and fervor—can fade into indistinctness. We can forget the power and provision of God, though they are continually open to us in our distresses and needs. We can think only in terms of here and now and lose sight of eternity and the rewards of living faithfully for Jesus.

Early in his letter to the Ephesians, Paul demonstrated exactly what it means to pray for the saints: "[For I always pray] the God of our Lord Jesus Christ, the Father of Glory, that He may grant you a spirit of wisdom and revelation—of insight into mysteries and secrets—in the [deep and intimate] knowledge of Him, by having the eyes of your heart flooded with light, so that you can know and understand the hope to which He has called you and how rich is His glorious inheritance in the saints— His set-apart ones. And [so that you can know and understand] what is the immeasurable and unlimited and surpassing greatness of His power in and for us who believe, as demonstrated in the working of His mighty strength, which He exerted in Christ when He raised Him from the dead and seated Him at His [own] right hand in the heavenly [places]" (Ephesians 1:17-20, Amplified Bible).

God's children face a spiritual enemy. God's children face situations that are too big and too complicated for them. And God's children need the prayers of one another to survive in this spiritual battle. God does not intend that we stand alone. He intends that we derive much strength from one another through prayer and encouragement. To experience that, we need to open our hearts to one another, confess our faults, share our struggles, acknowledge our weakness, give our testimonies, and name our requests so we can pray effectively and specifically for one another.

Spiritual victory is not a private matter. No one is intended to fight as a lone warrior. We are brothers and sisters, members of one body, and we need one another. When we fight alone, when we weep alone, when no one knows what we face, we are likely to fall alone. God wants us to stand together!

"And watching thereunto with all persever-ance." The enemy is sly, and the enemy is persistent. This calls for alertness on our part, not only for our own safety, but also for the safety of one another. We are indeed "our brother's keeper." His peril is our peril, for if he falls, we are more in danger of falling.

This means that sometimes we will stand by one another, literally, and sometimes in prayer at incon-venient times. In warfare, if a soldier sees his fellow soldier in danger at two o'clock in the morning, he does not say, "Well, I hope he makes it." Rather, he jumps to his aid. We are in a battle with far more consequences than any earthly battle ever fought. Sometimes we pray in the night. Sometimes we go to be with our fellow Christians when we would rather be sleeping or working or relaxing. We watch over one another "with all perseverance." We don't want the enemy to get the advantage at any time with any of our comrades.

O Father, teach us to pray! Teach us to pray in the Spirit. Teach us to pray for the saints. Teach us to be watchful in prayer. Teach us to perse-vere in prayer. In the daily round of living, may prayer be always rising from our hearts—our requests, our thanks, and our offerings of praise. Enable us to pray in accord with Your purposes. May Your will be done on earth as it is in Heaven! Give us Your heart as we put into words the needs of Your people. Grant us the humility to share our needs with others and the commitment to bring their needs to You. Enable us to stand shoulder to shoulder with our fellow warriors. Open our eyes always to the help available to us from heaven, and may You be pleased to answer our requests for Your glory! Amen.

Those who would live the victorious life, must do so with the awareness that our victory has been secured by Jesus. Our hope of winning against the enemy does not depend on our strength, but on His, and on our laying hold of Him.

In Christ, the victory is assured no matter what our earthly circumstances. In Him, though we may be "accounted as sheep for the slaughter," we are safe. Paul's resounding words are, "Nay, in all these things we are MORE THAN CONQUERORS through him that loved us" (Romans 8:36, 37). Amen and amen!

Christian Light Publications, Inc., is a nonprofit, conservative Mennonite publishing company providing Christ-centered, Biblical literature including books, Gospel tracts, Sunday school materials, summer Bible school materials, and a full curriculum for Christian day schools and homeschools. Though produced primarily in English, some books, tracts, and school materials are also available in Spanish.

For more information about the ministry of CLP or its publications, or for spiritual help, please contact us at:

Christian Light Publications, Inc.
P. O. Box 1212
Harrisonburg, VA 22803-1212

Telephone—540-434-0768
Fax—540-433-8896
E-mail—info@clp.org
www.clp.org